The Beast watches Beauty at supper (p. 105).

Hammond Collection

BEAUTY AND THE BEAST

Diary of a Film

BY JEAN COCTEAU

translated by
RONALD DUNCAN

with a new Introduction by
GEORGE AMBERG
Late Chairman, Department of Cinema Studies,
New York University

Dover Publications Inc., New York

This Dover edition, first published in 1972, is an
unabridged translation of Cocteau's book *La Belle
et la Bête: Journal d'un film,* originally published
in French by J. B. Janin, Paris, in 1947 *(dépôt légal
1946).*
The present English translation is a revision of
the one originally published as *Diary of a Film (La
Belle et la Bête)* by Dennis Dobson Limited, London,
in 1950, in their series "International Theatre and
Cinema" (general editor, Herbert Marshall) . The
present edition is published by special arrangement
with Dobson Books Ltd.
A new Introduction has been written specially for
this edition by George Amberg. All the illustrations
are from stills in the collection of Robert M.
Hammond, to whom the publisher expresses his
gratitude.

International Standard Book Number: 0-486-22776-6
Library of Congress Catalog Card Number: 77-130640

Manufactured in the United States of America
Dover Publications, Inc.
180 Varick Street
New York, N. Y. 10014

introduction
to the Dover edition

Diary of a Film covers the making of *Beauty and the Beast*, one of Cocteau's most accomplished cinematic creations. The film's pictorial glamor—the flawless composite of Cocteau's inspiration, Bérard's design and Alekan's photography—accounts for its lasting popularity. Yet, while it has charm and beauty, elegance and good manners, much like a well-made ballet, it is mostly glossy surface, reflecting little but itself. The incredible difficulties under which the production of this film suffered from beginning to end, so thoroughly documented in the *Diary*, were possibly not only an accidental accumulation of adverse circumstances; they suggest a more profound malaise. There prevails a climate of melancholy that is not wholly in the nature of a subject which, true to expectation, moves with certainty toward a happy ending. In an effort to avoid any suspicious traces of "poetic poetry," Cocteau went perhaps too far in the opposite direction, creating a glacial air of emotional detachment. Some critics, conscious of an apparent incongruity, have observed that the film's clean, sharp-edged precision conflicts with the conventional notion of a fairy tale. Cocteau would have argued that exactly the opposite was true and that, in fact, the critical reservations were missing a crucial point.

Actually, fairy tales are always exact and particular in the description of witches, dragons and monsters in the same spirit and for the same reason that the devils and angels in a religious painting are portrayed to appear real. Cocteau himself has frequently insisted that it is essential for the viability and credibility of the creatures of our imagination that their presumed existence be scrupulously authenticated. In *Beauty and the Beast*, "the characters of this film obey the rule of fairy stories. Nothing surprises them in a world to which matters are admitted as normal of which the

most insignificant would upset the mechanics of our world."
Granting that fairy-tale characters are archetypes or stereotypes,
they must assume at least a distinct make-believe personality, the
more so as their function is inflexible, allowing for no subtle
nuances between black and white, good and evil. Because it passes
through a process of gradual, psychological transformation, the
Beast emerges, paradoxically, as the sole human creature in an
artificial world. And not by accident either. Cocteau describes how
he "made of him a monster which, instead of being awful, remains
seductive, with that kind of a monster's seductiveness in which one
feels at once the man and the beast." Thanks to Jean Marais's
moving performance and Christian Bérard's extraordinary make-
up and mask design, the Beast absorbs almost all the feeling and
compassion that are otherwise painfully frustrated.

The film was dear to Cocteau because he had visions of an otherworldly creation of pure, transcendent beauty. He felt, and indeed
he was, in sufficient control of the medium to translate his vision
into images of exquisite "reality." It was a daring exercise in style.
Cocteau's very personal notion of reality provides a key to the
film's unique style, which he chose to call "documentary." He
objects to any form of obscurity or vagueness, suggesting instead
that "mystery exists only in precise things," an aesthetic position
related to Surrealism. There are many corroborating statements,
especially in his published conversation on the cinema. He believes
that the "strength of a film resides in its 'truthism' [*vérisme*], I mean
in its showing us things instead of telling them. Thus they are made
to exist as facts, even if these facts rest upon the unreal or upon
what the public is not accustomed to seeing." Furthermore, "there
is nothing we cannot convey in a film, provided we succeed in
investing it with a force of expression sufficient for changing our
phantasms into undeniable facts." And finally, "all films are
realistic in that they *show* things instead of suggesting them
in words."

Cocteau's frequent excursions into the cinema represent, by his
own definition, not a departure from but rather an extension of his
poetic endeavor. The difference is in the medium or genre rather
than in intention or creative impulse; for him, the cinema "is only
one medium of expression among others," though indeed one
mastered with supreme skill. His answer to the sceptic is that "the
function has created the organ." The astonishing control of the

medium his films display, is the concomitant of a particular vision that inspired him. If Cocteau's vision is poetic, which is our presupposition, the means he employs to convey it are unorthodox and deliberately anti-poetic. His favorite example is the work of the painter Vermeer, whose homey and familiar subjects are endowed with magical power, "peopled with another world than the world he represents. The subject of his picture is only a pretext, a vehicle by which the universe of the fantastic is expressed." This intelligence gives meaning to Cocteau's frequent use of such terms as "realistic" or "documentary" in connection with motion pictures that would be normally considered "poetic" or "fantastic."

Elaborating on the same principle, the *Diary* reads, "People have decided once and for all that fuzziness is poetic. Now, . . . in my eyes poetry is precision, number." Throughout the *Diary*, as elsewhere in his writings, there is ample evidence of Cocteau's pervading fear of falling into the trap of poetic conventions, be they literary or cinematic. It is implied in such information as, "my method is simple: not to aim at poetry. That must come of its own accord. The mere whispered mention of its name frightens it away." Similarly, on another occasion, he said, "the true poet rarely bothers about poetry. Does a gardener perfume his roses?" While all this is to the point, the *Diary* also contains one puzzling, even misleading statement in which the author explains, "this *had* to be attempted once: a poet telling a story through the medium of the camera." There is no accounting for this deliberate mystification. Actually, *Beauty and the Beast* was the second film he directed, not counting the several preceding productions on which he had decisively collaborated, including the excessively romantic story of *The Eternal Return*. More significantly, at least one previous film, *The Blood of a Poet*, was an elaborate, metaphorical self-portrait of the artist as a poet—told precisely "through the medium of the camera."

Cocteau's versatility as a film-maker is astonishing, not to say disconcerting. There is neither thematic nor stylistic cohesion in his cinematic oeuvre—although his identification with the Orphic myth prevails and recurs over the years, beginning with the first effort in *Blood of a Poet* and fittingly ending with *The Testament of Orpheus*, thirty years later. All his productions, fantastic or naturalistic, are copiously documented with commentaries and explications. Strangely enough, for all the minute information contained in the *Diary*, he mentions only once what supposedly inspired him to film the popular story of *Beauty and the Beast*. "I chose that particular fable," he wrote, "because it corresponded to my personal mythology." The finished product hardly bears out the poet's contention. Of all his motion pictures, *Beauty and the Beast* is the least mythological as well as the least autobiographical one. Except for the scathing irony of the happy ending, the film avoids the personal clues and allusions that abound in his other works. The climax, however, allows room for speculation. The deliberate Disney banality of the too-handsome Prince Charming threatens to break the delicate fabric that the poet had so skillfully woven. The pat ending, traditionally so right and predictable, disregards the dark undercurrent of genuine pathos and suffering that had made the Beast enduring and endearing. His magic transformation and ascension leave a feeling almost of regret and disappointment — and of wonder. After the metamorphosis, the *Diary* reads, "this Prince Charming looks extraordinarily like Avenant [her former swain], and the likeness worries Beauty. She seems to miss the kind Beast . . . ."

As was surely the author's purpose, the *Diary* reveals everything the film disguises, possibly more than the reader asks for. It is a strange document, reminiscent in its unrestrained candor if not in scope, of Rousseau's *Confessions*. The parallel is inescapable. Like his great compatriot, Cocteau is presenting an unflattering self-portrait. In both instances there is the obsessive self-observation that omits no detail, however private; there is the same excessive preoccupation with health problems, however repugnant; there is the complaint of not being properly appreciated, however exaggerated; and there is, most of all, the compelling urge to justify their every thought and action, indeed their very selves, however remote from public concern. Owing to the genius of the authors, their revelations transcend the limitations of the factual content. A very real pathos is common to both because they are men of stature and accomplishment. Unlike Rousseau's monolithic monument, Cocteau's confessions are dispersed throughout his whole oeuvre, sometimes metaphorically, most of the time explicitly, as in the *White Paper* and *Opium. Diary of a Film* is, by definition, of considerably less ambitious compass. Primarily, it records the events accompanying the production of *Beauty and the Beast* in regular entries from August 26, 1945, to June 1, 1946.

The study of the *Diary* would be greatly increased in comprehension and meaning by simultaneously consulting the film's scenario, available in a critical, annotated edition.* Aside from the added literary merit of the dialogue, the script provides accurate, very detailed description of the action, the settings, costumes, props, as well as blocking, framing and camera positions. It is enormously instructive to follow scene by scene in the *Diary* the problems the director encountered and the ingenuity with which he resolved them. For in the actual shooting he adhered very closely to the scenario, even to the extent of trying to beat the weather in order to capture the appropriate atmosphere. Seen side by side, the documents confirm that the director had visualized the realization of his film as severely pared of all romantic-sentimental embellishments and clichés. The only remaining, unequivocally romantic symbol is the red rose that was stolen from the Beast. In this connection, the *Diary* notes, "it is very probable that this rose is one of the jaws of a trap which will now ensnare Beauty through all eternity." Yet this hint at an inescapable design of life and death, of moving forces beyond human control, occurs significantly outside the realm of the film, implicitly recognizing that the story is not dealing with humans. The motion picture proper, mystery, magic and all, is straightforward narrative, almost literally following the original fairy tale, appended to this edition.

On reading the *Diary*, which is wholly authentic and truthful, one is simply amazed at the superhuman control Cocteau exerted over the whole production. Ill-fated from the very outset, it started at a time of exceptional difficulties. France, only recently liberated and not nearly recovered from the hardships of war and occupation, was hardly geared to film production. Technical equipment was scarce, obsolete or in a bad state of disrepair; raw stock was at a premium and unreliable; studio space was doled out by the hour; the electric power was turned off frequently and unpredictably; the task of collecting some plain white sheets created a major crisis; the carcass of a deer was near-impossible to procure. Each shooting day provided its own, particular catastrophe, though also the satisfaction of having overcome yet another obstacle. In telling

*Beauty and the Beast . . . , Edited and Annotated by Robert M. Hammond, New York University Press, 1970 (a bilingual edition, the English translation being by Professor Hammond). The Hammond book provides full explanations of scenes and sequences (such as the "draper farce") of which Cocteau describes the filming in *Diary of a Film* but which are not included in any known print of *Beauty and the Beast*.

this story, Cocteau lavishes well-deserved praise on the devotion and loyalty of his artistic collaborators and his technical crew. For in addition to those innumerable practical problems, most of the key people were afflicted with an almost unbelievable series of accidents and illnesses, to say nothing of Cocteau's own miserable state of health. More than once, the cumulative weight of all those mishaps, miseries and crises threatened the continuation of the work. When it was finally ready for its first public viewing, Cocteau's weary comment was, "The only thing I could see in it were the memories attached to every foot of it and the suffering it had caused me."

It would be quite wrong, though, to conclude on this mournful note. The *Diary* is not merely a tale of woes, however much those woes may have interfered with the smooth progression of the work. For page after page, through the whole tale, runs the leitmotif of an indomitable determination to complete the task and to complete it well. This is precisely what eventually happened. The end product, the film itself, shows not the slightest traces of the labor that went into it or of the suffering that accompanied it. If we trust the testimony of successful artists, all creative work is an ordeal while it is in progress. It is neither demeaned nor ennobled by baring or avowing the particulars of the working process. The production of *Beauty and the Beast* turned out to be impeccable: clean, smooth, polished, stylish, and entirely of a piece. The source of these positive qualities is also contained in the *Diary*. Cocteau had no reservations whatever about revealing usually closely guarded professional secrets, the technical tricks with which he achieved his magic effects, the way he worked his visual wonders. These passages are endlessly fascinating, even for the layman who is privileged to witness the birth of an illusion and the creation of art.

GEORGE AMBERG

list of illustrations

Since this book is written in the form of an intimate diary, Jean Cocteau sometimes takes it for granted that the names of his friends and associates are familiar to the reader. As this is not always so, the list of credits below will be helpful to the reader.

THE CAST

Jean Marais (Jeannot)	The Beast · Avenant · Ardent (Prince Charming)
Josette Day	Beauty
Marcel André	The Merchant
Mila Parely*	Adélaïde ⎱ (Beauty's sisters)
Nane Germon	Félicie ⎰
Michel Auclair	Ludovic (Beauty's brother)
Doudou	Diana
Diot	Jean Marais's stand-in
Carrier	A bit player

THE TECHNICIANS

G. R. Aldo	Stills
Henri Alekan*	Camera
Hagop Arakelian (Ara)*	Make-up
Georges Auric	Music
Christian Bérard	Décor and Costumes
Bouboule	Assistant Sound
Carné	Properties
René Clément	Technical Advisor
Emile Darbon	Production Manager
Marcel Escoffier	Wardrobe
Claude Ibéria	Editing
Jacques Lebreton	Sound Engineer
Lucienne (Lucile)	Continuity Girl
Raymonde Méresse	Lights
Moulaert	Settings
André Paulvé	Producer
Roger Rogelys*	Stage Manager
Rouzenat	Effects (Sound)
Tiquet	Assistant Camera
Moulouk	Marais's dog
Jacinthe	A cat

*These names appear with accents in some publications: Parély, Alékan, Arakélian, Rogélys.

The monkey in the mirror (p. 68).

Hammond Collection

from J. Cocteau, Beauty & the Beast: Diary of a Film, tr. R. Duncan, Dover, 1972 (originally published in Paris in 1947)

prologue

In a land none other than that vague country of fairy tales, there lives a merchant who has been ruined by losing his ships, laden with merchandise, in a storm. He has three daughters and a son. The latter, called Ludovic, is a charming scamp, always getting into trouble with his friend Avenant. Two of the daughters, Félicie and Adélaïde, are very wicked, and have made a slave out of the third daughter, Beauty, a real Cinderella of the family.

In this household of bickerings and shouts, Beauty serves at table and polishes the floor. Avenant loves her. He asks her to marry him, but she refuses. She wants to remain unmarried and live with her father.

This father, a good man if a little weak, has just received some good news. One of his cargo ships has reached harbor. People of fashion who previously ignored him, again make their calls. Again Félicie and Adélaïde clamor for dresses and jewels. Ludovic borrows money from a usurer. As her father rides away to the harbor, Beauty asks for a rose, "for none grow here."

That's where the story begins. The sisters laugh at her request which she made rather than seem to ask for nothing. And the merchant departs on horseback over the highways.

At the harbor he learns that his creditors have got there first, and seized the ship and all his goods, leaving him nothing, not even enough to pay for lodging at an inn of the port. He must ride back through the thick forest, though night has already fallen and a mist is rising.

It is obvious that the poor man will lose his way. He hunts for the path, leading his horse by its bridle, and he sees a light. Branches part. He enters a bridle-path. The branches close behind him. Gradually he makes his way through an immense empty castle, bristling with riddles: candles which light themselves and statues which seem to be alive. Worn out, he falls asleep at a table that is hardly reassuring despite the fruit and wine on it. A far-off roar and the death cry of some animal wake him. He flies for his life. He loses his way again, and then, finding himself in an arbor of roses, he remembers Beauty's request. A rose is now the only gift he will be able to bring. He picks one. Thereupon, the echo which had answered his cries of "Hello! Is there anyone there?" becomes a terrible voice roaring: "Who's there!"

He turns and sees the Beast, who looks like a great nobleman, except that his hands and face are those of a beast of prey. Whereupon the Beast pronounces the mysterious postulate of the story: "You have stolen my roses, therefore you must die. Unless one of your daughters consents to die in your place."

It is very probable that this rose is one of the jaws of a trap which will now ensnare Beauty through all eternity.

The father is given a horse called Magnificent to ride home on. All he has to do is to whisper in its ear: "Go where I go, Magnificent —go, go, go!" And no doubt this horse is the other jaw of the trap.

The sisters are furious. Beauty offers to go to the Beast, Father refuses. Avenant is angry but, in the middle of a violent scene, the old man collapses, and Beauty, taking advantage of the uproar, escapes through the night. Mounting Magnificent, she whispers the magic password, and gallops toward her martyrdom.

But once in the Beast's castle, Beauty finds a different fate from the one she expected. The trap is working perfectly. The Beast surrounds her with luxury and kindness, for though he looks ferocious, he has a kind heart. He suffers because of his ugliness and his ugliness moves one to pity.

Gradually Beauty will also be moved by it, but her father is ill. A magic mirror proves this to her. She too falls ill. The Beast, finally, opens his trap slightly. Beauty is given eight days in which to go home to her father, under a promise that she will return to the castle. The Beast has several magic objects which are the ultimate secrets of his power. To show his trust in Beauty he gives them to her: his glove which will take her where she wishes, the golden key which opens the pavilion of Diana. There his real treasure is piled, which no one must touch, neither he nor she, till his death.

"I know your heart," he says to Beauty, "and this key will be the pledge of your return."

Once home, Beauty's jewels excite the jealousy of her sisters. They try flattery on her, and then, to dupe her, feign tears to move her to pity and so prevent her from returning to the castle, for they want to turn her into a servant again. By this trick Beauty is made to break her promise, and then no longer dares to return. Félicie and Adélaïde steal her golden key. Magnificent arrives. He is the only magic object that the Beast did not give away. That and the mirror which he bears. Without doubt these have been sent as a last appeal from her forsaken love. It is not Beauty, however, who rides Magnificent to the castle, but Ludovic and Avenant, whom the sisters have persuaded to kill the Beast and steal his treasure. They give them the golden key.

Looking into the magic mirror, Beauty sees the Beast weeping. She is all alone. She puts on the glove. She is at the castle. Where is the Beast? She calls him, she runs about looking for him, and finds him beside the lake dying.

Meanwhile Ludovic and Avenant have reached the pavilion of Diana. Fearing some trap, they dare not use the key. So they climb onto the roof of the pavilion and through the skylight they see the treasure, a statue of Diana and snow circulating as it used to do in those glass balls which one had as a child. Ludovic is afraid. Avenant breaks the panes of glass. He is a doubting Thomas: "It is only glass," he cries. Ludovic [sic] will let himself down, holding his friend's hands; he will jump down into the pavilion and will make his way as best he can afterwards. At the lake Beauty is lamenting. She begs the Beast to listen to her. The Beast murmurs: "Too late." Beauty is almost at the point of saying: "I love you."

Back at the pavilion, Avenant is letting himself down through the broken glass. Just then the statue of Diana moves, raises her bow, aims. The arrow strikes him in the back. Ludovic, terrified, sees Avenant's face contorted with agony as it turns into the Beast's. He falls. At that very moment the Beast must have been transformed under Beauty's eyes as they filled with love. It was only this loving look from a young girl which could break the curse. Beauty jumps back, for now a Prince Charming stands before her, bowing and explaining the marvel.

This Prince Charming looks extraordinarily like Avenant, and the likeness worries Beauty. She seems to miss the kind Beast a little, and to be a little afraid of this unexpected Avenant. But the end of a fairy story is the end of a fairy story. Beauty is docile.

And it is with the Prince with three faces that she flies to a kingdom where, as he says: "You will be a great queen, you will find your father, and your sisters will carry your train."

the diary

I have decided to write a diary of *La Belle et la Bête* as the work on the film progresses. After a year of preparations and difficulties, the moment has now come to grapple with a dream. Apart from the numerous obstacles which exist in getting a dream onto celluloid, the problem is to make a film within the limits imposed by a period of austerity. But perhaps these limitations may stimulate imagination, which is often lethargic when all means are placed at its disposal.

Everybody knows the story by Madame Leprince de Beaumont, a story often attributed to Perrault, because it is found next to "Peau d'Ane" between those bewitching covers of the *Bibliothèque Rose*.[1]

The postulate of the story requires faith, the faith of childhood. I mean that one must believe implicitly at the very beginning and not question the possibility that the mere picking of a rose might lead a family into adventure, or that a man can be changed into a beast, and vice versa. Such enigmas offend grown-ups who are readily prejudiced, proud of their doubt, armed with derision. But I have the impudence to believe that the cinema which depicts the impossible is apt to carry conviction, in a way, and may be able to put a "singular" occurrence into the plural.

It is up to us (that is, to me and my unit—in fact, one entity) to avoid those impossibilities which are even more of a jolt in the midst of the improbable than in the midst of reality. For fantasy has its own laws which are like those of perspective. You may not bring what is distant into the foreground, or render fuzzily what

[1] [Standard collection of children's literature with pink cloth covers.]
(Throughout this book, numbered footnotes in brackets contain information added by the publisher in 1971, whereas footnotes introduced by asterisks are translations of Cocteau's original footnotes to the text.)

is near. The vanishing lines are impeccable and the orchestration so delicate that the slightest false note jars. I am not speaking of what I have achieved, but of what I shall attempt within the means at my disposal.

My method is simple: not to aim at poetry. That must come of its own accord. The mere whispered mention of its name frightens it away. I shall try to build a table. It will be up to you then to eat at it, to examine it or to chop it up for firewood.

Sunday, August 26, 1945.

After a year of every sort of preparation and difficulty, I am going to start shooting tomorrow. It would be stupid to complain of the type of difficulties inherent in such a task, for I think that our work compels us to indulge in daydreams, to dream the most beautiful dreams. And what's more, it will give us the opportunity to do what we like with human time, which is normally so painful to live through minute by minute, in order. To break time up, turn it inside out and upside down, is a real triumph over the inevitable.

To the tangle of meetings about scenery and costumes, and to the search for the exteriors, I have had to add daily visits to doctors, to say nothing of those of the nurses to me. For as a result of sunburn and bad mosquito bites, I came back from my holiday with two carbuncles on my chest.

This wearing existence did not tire me in the least. The film possessed me, sustained me, made me insensible, took me from the weak anguish which idleness causes me, and compelled me to leave a room where hostile waves paralyze me and keep me from writing.

Watching Christian Bérard at work is an extraordinary sight. At Paquin's, surrounded by tulle and ostrich feathers, smeared with charcoal, covered with perspiration and stains, his beard on fire, his shirt hanging out, he gives to luxury a profound significance. Between his small ink-stained hands, the costumes cease to be the usual disguises and take on the arrogant youth of fashion. I mean, he makes us realize that a costume is not merely a costume but something dependent on many circumstances which change quickly and compel you to change with them. Men and women dressed by Bérard look as though they lived at a definite place, in a definite period, and not as though they were going to a fancy dress ball.

By a miracle, he has succeeded in merging the style of Vermeer with that of the Gustave Doré illustrations to Perrault's stories in the big book with the red and gold cover.

What impresses me in these big dressmaking houses is the love, care and grace with which the women work. Three or four spinsters, who used to embroider theater costumes for Gaby Deslys and Ida Rubinstein,[2] have a real genius which will die with them.

This morning, in the farmyard at Rochecorbon (where I am shooting) I saw these dresses hanging in the sun in an enormous wide-open box, side by side, like Bluebeard's wives. There was nothing left to them. To come alive, they must find their soul, and the soul of a dress is a body. We reached Tours at five o'clock yesterday. Paris was covered by clouds. Gradually on the way out the sky cleared, and the clouds became ruffled and thin, forming little groups like those in the paintings which inspire me. The Loire flowed through Touraine flat beneath the sun-bleached sky. Rochecorbon—I again found the tiny manor, built below the level of the road, which I had luckily stumbled across when first looking for a location. The renting agency had pointed it out to us, along with fifty others. The gate by the road didn't look very promising. We very nearly didn't bother to get out of the car. Then all at one glance I *recognized*, down to the smallest detail, the exact setting that I was afraid I would have to build. The man who lives there looks exactly like the merchant in the story, and his son said to me: "If you had come by yesterday you would have heard your own voice. I was playing your poetry records over to my father." On top of this, the iron rings for tethering the horses are made in the shape of a fabulous beast. Here are the windows of the wicked sisters, the doors, the staircase, the wash-house, the orchard, the stables, the kennel, the dog, the watering cans, the tomatoes ripening on the window sills, the vegetables, the firewood, the spring, the chicken-run, the ladders. Everything is already there. The interior is as good as the exterior, and this hidden rightness shines through the walls. All that we have to do is to move the sun, that is, to move ourselves several times per scene so that we get its light. That was our job for the day, in the midst of the assistant

[2] [Gaby Deslys (1881–1920) was a musical comedy performer fêted in Paris and on Broadway; she generally wore very elaborate costumes. Ida Rubenstein (*c.* 1885–1960) was a noted Russian-born classical dancer who worked with Diaghilev and independently (it was she who commissioned Ravel's *Boléro*).]

cameramen, the electricians, the set-builders, unrolling their cables
and fitting up their workshops, some outside and others in the
barns. At eight o'clock tomorrow morning I shall set up the scene
of the drying sheets. I shall shoot this scene first because the
direction of the light is right for it, and we are still waiting for
certain equipment.

Monday morning, 7:30.

   This morning I must begin to solidify, to model in space and
time, something that I have long dreamed about, imagined, seen
on an invisible screen. And I must do this in bits, backwards,
forwards, before, after, in such a way that the editing can give it
continuity and life. We must set up these lanes of drying sheets with
the perspectives of the theater at Vicenza,[3] set them up in a place
other than where they are, in order to obtain shots against the light
and to follow the shifting spotlights of the sun. We must remember
to wet the sheets so as to make them more transparent. We must
plant clothes props that will stand up straight, split bamboos for
clothespins and counter too much shadow with lamps. We must
avoid the foreground terrain, which won't match the background
of the orchard, and then replant this linen décor in the orchard,
where Beauty goes and sits when Avenant draws back the first
sheet as if it were a theater curtain, revealing the bench against its
background of white lanes. We must even remember never to
mention the word "rope," which is taboo in film work under pain
of a fine. It is all such a mixture of realism and fantasy that I could
not sleep and exhausted myself trying to foresee the least difficulty.
   The artists—Mila Parely, Nane Germon, Marais, Michel Auclair
—will come at nine. I shall make them up, dress them, dirty them,
rip their clothes, until they look right for a story where dirt is not
dirt, where, as Goethe says, truth and reality contradict each other
(like the shadow falling the wrong way in the engraving by
Rubens).[4] We shall lunch on the set.

---

3 [The Teatro Olimpico, Palladio's last work, begun in 1580, famous for its optical effects.]

4 [This refers to one of Eckermann's conversations with Goethe (April 18, 1827), in which Goethe
uses a Rubens engraving with arbitrarily placed shadows as an example of an artistic truth "truer"
than reality.]

Monday evening, 7:30.

A tough beginning in wonderful weather which became overcast at about five o'clock. It was very sultry. I had to struggle
against the wine which the owner of the house forces me to drink,
in spite of there being water from a spring so clear that the animals
are deceived and take the trough to be empty. There are washing
places, streams and little waterfalls everywhere.

The décor is of the kind I must make with my own hands;
nobody can help me. Besides, the clothes props bent, the clothes
lines wouldn't get taut, the sheets were too short and there weren't
enough of them. The wind got up, making them billow, and ruined
their perspectives. The costumes stand out marvelously against the
walls of linen, and make fine shadows through them. But, by ill
luck, at five o'clock it clouded over and the stormy sky made me
stop work on the long shots with several actors and use lamps for
close-ups. Mila posed, posed, posed, lost her composure. The
camera developed a tremor. The electricians and workmen tried to
fix it, but couldn't, so we stopped. The written report I will submit
is all right for the firm, but as for me—my work has been interrupted in full flight. I was taking off. I came down again. I went
back to Tours worn out with fatigue, Vouvray and disappointment.
I had hoped that the fine weather would last, and that I could break
my normal rhythm and enjoy a rhythm of good luck. I was naïve.
The same difficulties pursue me, and as they appear each time from
a different angle they take me unawares.

Will we have any sun? Will we have a camera that works? Will
something else go wrong? I will try to get some sleep and wait.
Wait. That's how it is with films.

If I hadn't been so absorbed in this carnival booth work, I would
have enjoyed the sight of this orchard and this perfect little manor
house, enlivened by the actors bathing and making themselves up
outdoors around a huge kitchen table, and the workmen standing
and eating their lunch from planks laid across trestles.

Amiability. It's a dangerous weapon. The workmen like me;
they go out of their way for me. But for all that I always end up
working by myself. Carné, Christian, etc.—they get angry, make
demands and are obeyed. This evening after dinner I spoke to
Darbon. I told him that I thought it was almost a godsend that the
camera had broken down, for his set looked as though it had been

made out of handkerchiefs and walking-sticks, fit for some charade such as I sometimes improvise with Bérard in my room. I told him that it merely gave a crude idea which he must now realize, and that, whatever the sky was like tomorrow, I at least wanted to find a real set when I arrived, and not just a poet's theatrical improvisation.With that I went to bed. The sky is still overcast. I can just make out a few stars. The trees are restless. I'm told that the camera is working again, but it is possible that it still quivers imperceptibly. Nothing is worse than risking a take only to find out afterwards that it is out of focus. I shall be fretting about this on my second day.

Tuesday morning, 7 o'clock.

First thing, I look at the sky. It is overcast! Now we are going to be held up for days, with the actors all ready, and able to do nothing but play cards. Delannoy warned me that one must always stand at the ready in Touraine as the weather changes in an instant.

I wonder if it is not all to the good that it is cloudy now. For if it weren't I should probably be shooting with a hastily patched-up camera I could never be sure of. If the weather stays like this for a while, I may be able to get hold of another camera and also a better arrangement of the sheets (and a few more of them too).

What makes my task difficult in uncertain weather is the angle at which each planned shot must be taken. A break in the clouds won't permit me to take any shot I want. That depends on the position of the sun. In short, everyone must be prepared to act and to carry the electrical equipment either in front of the house, or behind it, or into the orchard, or into the barnyard. I've got the same unit that we used in *Baron Fantôme*,[5] willing and helpful. Everybody, down to the least workman, participates in the film, likes it, takes an interest in it and helps the artists in all sorts of ways. You can ask them and get them to do anything you like. Which is different from the theater, where the stage-hands keep to their dark wings, and have not the slightest interest in our work.

I was astonished to hear of the speed with which they work in America. René Clair tells me he takes from twelve to seventeen shots a day. He completed *I Married a Witch* in eight weeks. On the other hand, their labor union difficulties are even worse than ours.

[5] [Cocteau wrote the dialogue and played the title role in this 1943 film directed (and with screenplay by) Serge de Poligny.]

In his last picture,[6] after the completion of the job, he still needed a shot of five of his principals in a boat in mid-ocean. Since they were going to appear three hundred yards off, he decided to make extras stand-in with their costumes. The extras insisted on being paid the same salaries as the stars for whom they were doubling, and refused to go on unless the stars were also paid. This was impossible because the stars were working on other pictures and their union forbids them to have two contracts running at the same time. So he decided to replace the extras by painted silhouettes. Then the extras complained that the silhouettes were doing them out of work. The whole thing was impossible.

René Clair consulted a lawyer. The scene called for big waves. The lawyer told him that these waves would save the scene from being a washout. The shot would come under the union of stunt artists. This union alone would allow the scene to be shot without committing an offense of one kind or another.

3 o'clock.

Mila and Jean Marais brought my lunch to my room. An extraordinary luxury in this hotel (which is otherwise not so bad) though Josette thinks it's like some dive in Tananarive. It's still cloudy but breaking up here and there. The assistant cameramen are observing this play of light of varying intensity, their yellow glasses held to their eyes. If a medium intensity (veiled sunlight) continues, we can shoot. If it changes we must wait. I shall be on the set at a quarter to nine.

The sky was very grey and overcast this morning. The clouds weren't even moving. When we reached the set it looked like a flea market. I roused the workmen and ordered them to cut big planks to make X's, to place a third plank across the top and to hang the linen. Gradually this changed the look of things. The toy set became a real theater of linen and the clothes props broke up the flat surfaces in every direction. Alekan and his assistants tested the camera. They decided to try it out on a sort of geometrically checkered target, and to put a short length of film through it and watch through the view-finder to see if it still had a tremor. The question was how to develop ten yards of film on the spot, using

6 [The film referred to is *And Then There Were None* (1945), Clair's last Hollywood assignment. *I Married a Witch* was made in 1942.]

a test-bath in an improvised laboratory. The assistants managed to do it and I saw them washing their film in the wash-house. The camera works. A new one will arrive tomorrow. I hurried to set everything in position for the close-ups; for these I didn't need to spy out the slightest ray of sunlight. No sooner was I ready for the close-ups than the sky cleared and the sun shone. It was impossible to go back and jump to the scene of the Merchant's departure. We would need Josette, Marcel André, the horse, etc. . . . I went on, but now Alekan had to avoid the very sun that we were all waiting for, and hide it with planks—in short, prolong the earlier half-light, in which electricity plays the part of the sun.

Before the arrival of Clément, who is in Brittany finishing his film on the resistance of the railway workers[7] and has sent me his young brother, I must take care of everything myself, from pinning the sheets, tying up the clothes props, rounding up the chickens and driving them onto the set, making the lanes of sheets and preparing the perspective views between them. (One can't imagine what it is like in 1945 to hire twelve additional sheets. Roger Rogelys, the property man, has found nine for me with great difficulty. I had six before.) These alleys and wings of sheets are constructed as they are needed, but this makes another area bare so that I can't take a bird's-eye shot of the whole set. Perhaps it's just as well. If I had to describe this labyrinth of linen in words, I would attempt to get the reader lost in it, and this would no longer be the case if I lifted the lid and showed an aerial view of the jack-in-the-box in advance. I must avoid tracking shots. I must reveal these white corridors in successive shocks so that the spectator cannot tell whether the set is gigantic or tiny.

I'll leave the group shot of the sheets to the last and for that I'll get them back to their proper place at the back of the orchard; but I'll shoot the main sheet sequence elsewhere. This is a film-maker's privilege.

This afternoon I was almost drunk with fatigue, thirst, sheets, clothespins, clothes props, and I got muddled up. My poor head could no longer recall the continuity of the shots. Jean Marais kept me from ruin. He held out a life line to me, and got my ideas straightened out with astonishing patience and intuition.

Got home at eight o'clock. Dined with the unit and a lady

---

[7] [*La Bataille du rail* (1946), René Clément's first feature film, most of it filmed by Alekan, the *Beauty and the Beast* cinematographer.]

journalist. She was looking for anecdotes. But hearing us talk of cutting problems, perspectives and acting drove her mad. She must have been expecting the old chestnuts of a theater company. Now, luckily for me, the problems that interest me deeply also interest my artists. I cite them the case of A., the make-up man. He never takes the slightest interest in the shots, never looks at his work under the lights, never tries to perfect it. He sits far away from the set reading a paper, and thinks he's done enough because he has stuck on an eyelash, or powdered the back of someone's neck. The others put their whole back into it, and my cameraman listens to the advice of Aldo, the still photographer.

I'm terrified tomorrow morning will be overcast. I must finish this sheet scene with the nine o'clock sun on it. If the sun hides, I shall start setting up the Merchant going off on horseback. I can only start to shoot this scene at five o'clock, when the sun is shining obliquely on the back of the house. The worst of it is that that scene is a long one, what with the angles, platforms and scaffolds, and Marcel André has to be back in Paris before the others.

I was forgetting the airplanes. No sooner had we got the lights ready for the close-up of Mila than a plane from the school flew over us, looping the loop and ruining our sound. We telephoned the colonel of the school to have him stop the students from doing this somewhat expensive kind of frisking about. He promised he would.

Wednesday morning, 7 o'clock.

I have been awakened by a storm. The window is wide open opposite my bed. I see the mad trees sweeping the window frame, and the lightning flashing through them with magnificent anger and phosphorescent pallor. Thunder rolls down all the slopes of the sky.

May the clouds all dissolve and relieve us from this suffocating weight.

Even while I write the spectacle calms down. A pity. I was dreaming of a monster of a storm which would break the weather. If this is a stormy season, we are in the soup. It's strange that an enterprise as expensive as making films can be entirely at the mercy of the barometer.

Wednesday evening, 11 o'clock.

I'm so tired that I have to force myself to write even these few notes. A day of clouds, of rare bright spells, of half-light. With the greatest difficulty I have only been able to take seven shots, and these on the wing, surreptitiously, by surprise. The earth and sky were against me. After doing the shots of Michel and Jeannot, which last a second, but took an hour to prepare, I got ready for the shots of Josette–Mila–Nane and Marcel André behind the house. With the time change, seven o'clock is five o'clock by the sun. The sun appeared and disappeared. Planes shuttled across the sky. The camera trembled. (A new one had come from Paris. It imitated the eccentricities of the old one.) I was frantic (which is exhausting) but I tried to control myself so as not to upset the others. In Touraine it is best to shoot early in the morning and in the evening. But the idle hours in the middle of the day are the busy hours for the labor unions. Here the weather can change in a few minutes. The sun comes out when least expected, but if you wait for it, it never comes. It shines when you set up the scene, and disappears the moment you give the order to shoot. I got back to the hotel at seven o'clock. The Maison Paquin came down this evening from Paris and in one room they are fitting Jean Marais's costumes for the Beast and Prince Charming. The Beast is superb. The Prince is still not splendid enough, though it is in impeccable Perrault style. I have called the artists for 7:30 tomorrow morning. To bed.

An article in the Tours paper: misrepresentations in every line.

In a spirit of instinctive contradiction I am avoiding all camera movement, which is so much in fashion, and which the experts think indispensable. The scene with the linen is done flat, like a house of cards.

I'm finding it very difficult to make the artists understand that the style of the film needs a luster and a lack of naturalness that are supernatural. There is not much dialogue. They cannot permit the least fuzziness. The sentences are very short and precise. These sentences, which disconcert the actors and prevent them from "acting," when taken together form the cogs in a big machine, incomprehensible in detail. There are times when I am ashamed of imposing a discipline on them which they accept only out of confidence in me. Such confidence destroys my own and makes me fear I am not worthy of theirs.

A Rochecorbon exterior.
The Merchant leaving for
the harbor (p. 15).

Hammond Collection

The Rochecorbon linen set. Ludovic (Michel Auclair) with the watering cans; the shadow of a sister on a sheet (p. 15).

Hammond Collection

Thursday morning, 7 o'clock.

I woke up with a start in the night. It was raining. I had suddenly realized a mistake I had made, which I must correct without anybody noticing it. If they did they would lose confidence in me. I am not a real director and probably never shall be. I get too interested in what is happening. I begin to watch the action as though it were a play. I become a part of the audience and then I forget all about the continuity. I forgot to film the beginning of Marcel André's movement when he is about to mount his horse. So that we can still use that shot, I shall have to cut to Nane Germon at the window. She will say her lines again and then leave the window, so that Marcel in the next cut can start his movement from the edge of the frame. I shall finish his movement behind the horse when he mounts it and says, "And you, Beauty, what shall I bring you?"

If Clément were here I wouldn't make that kind of mistake again. He must be having terrible weather in Brittany. He should be here by now. On top of this, Marcel André has to leave in five days, and the weather's so uncertain it prevents me from finishing his scenes. It's still raining this morning but there is a chance that the sun may come out later. In Touraine the weather changes completely with extraordinary rapidity.

7 : 30 in the evening.

First day that I have actually done what I wanted to do. Splendid sunshine and clouds. We took advantage of the clouds after lunch to work behind the house, and to produce evening effects by using lamps.

This morning we nearly lost the little time that we'd gained on our schedule owing to the flying school students looping the loop above us. Darbon went to the center to see the officers. They paid us a visit at ten o'clock. One of them is Mangin's son.[8] They've promised to make the pilots fly further off.

I've nearly finished the linen sequence. With a bit of luck I should be through with it tomorrow, between nine and one o'clock. (Ludovic and his watering cans; Mila's shadow; the arrival of Beauty, dressed like a princess, against the backdrop of sheets disclosed by Jean Marais, who lifts up the first sheet as though it

[8] [The famous father was General Charles Marie Emmanuel Mangin (1866-1925), defender of Verdun in 1916 and victor at Villers-Cotterets in 1918.]

were a stage curtain to reveal the perspectives behind the bench.)

In order to make sure of Mila's and Nane's laughter in the close-up (on Josette's line, "Bring me a rose"), I asked Aldo to dress himself up as a "widow woman." He made up his face under a veil, and wore long blond curls made of wood shavings. He was grotesque and looked like old Bijou.[9] I pushed him out in front of them after the clapper boy. They told me they laughed because they didn't find him funny.

Tomorrow, after the linen, I shall go on to the orchard and do the scenes of Beauty appearing with her father, to link up the sheet settings with those of the house. Lebreton is recording sounds of chickens and running water for me, so that the background noises have the correct atmosphere.

The horse, Aramis, arrived with his master from Paris at four o'clock. He looks like Rommel's horse which Montgomery rides. He's a white Arab and kneels down and rears like a wave crowned with foam. I'll keep his circus harness, for it is absolutely right for the style of a children's book. I've asked his owner to send his false tail. Have seen the sedan chairs (too heavy and too clean). Have seen the crossbows (which don't work). But I won't get worked up anymore. When I do so, it's done deliberately in order to galvanize people and get the best out of them.

Friday evening, 8 o'clock.

Accident to Mila. She was trying to ride Aramis. He reared, or she made him rear. I was taking a shot of Josette. Meanwhile Mila was in a bathing suit; she basked in the sun, washed her hair in the wash-house and was just taking Aramis for a walk through the alfalfa. In front of the house, where none of us could see her, she must have tried to make this circus pony rear, by reining up. The horse fell back on top of her. It's a miracle she isn't dead. They've taken her over to Tours. She's very brave and makes light of it. But I don't suppose she'll be able to work for some time, nor does she yet realize the extent of her injuries as she's still suffering from shock. A reaction will probably set in. Her right leg has only superficial injuries.

It was beautifully fresh this morning. Sun shining, but the planes

[9][Very probably refers to the bejeweled and bedizened denizen of Montmartre immortalized in a Brassaï photo of 1932.]

In the linen décor, Beauty (Josette Day), dressed as a princess, recounts her adventures to Ludovic, Avenant (Jean Marais) and her father the Merchant (Marcel André) (p. 17).

Hammond Collection

A Rochecorbon exterior. Beauty shows her necklace to Adélaïde (Mila Parely) as Félicie (Nane Germon) and the others look on.

Hammond Collection

still there. Alekan was perched up as though on a tightrope and could only just keep his balance by moving very carefully. As soon as he was ready to shoot, it clouded over, a plane went by, a dog barked, guinea fowls drowned the actresses' voices, or the sound went wrong.

After an anti-diet lunch with the owners, I returned to the linen scene. Josette's sky-blue dress was ravishing in this very simple white setting.

To explain this background I make her say: "Who has done my washing?" Avenant replies, "We have," then she adds, "The sheets are badly hung and are trailing on the ground."

I returned to the hotel utterly exhausted. We are all going to dine at a country inn on the banks of the Cher. But it's difficult finding a road where debris doesn't block the car. Another anti-diet meal. I try with Alekan to solve the head-splitting problem of shots which will allow us not to use Mila and which will let us finish with Marcel André. I would have liked to take the crossbow scene which opens the film tomorrow morning, but all we could find at the Tours museum are some very heavy bows which are quite unworkable.

Marais has got a boil coming on his thigh.

Saturday evening, 8 o'clock.

Mila's better. Nane stayed with her. The masseur worked over her and allowed her to take a bath. Although she still walks bow-legged, that doesn't stop her laughing at herself and at everything else.

A good day. Emile Darbon complains that I don't get on with the schedule quickly enough but keep stopping to take extra shots, which the company haven't allowed for. But it's these extras, the inspiration of the moment, which enliven and enrich a film. I have not yet taken an insignificant shot. Each one pleased me and added to the meaning of the film. I took one today of a sort of open cart-shed full of ladders, ploughs, ploughshares, pitchforks, baskets, firewood and ropes. Beauty, Ludovic and Avenant sit here when they ask about the Beast: "Does it walk on four legs?" etc.

I decided to do this shot because it was overcast, and I could almost use studio lighting on it. But it took such a long time to

dress Josette and do her hair that, by the time she was ready, the
sun was out and I found myself having to use awnings to hide our
precious sunlight. Josette's grace and sensitive acting astonish me.
My short lines suit her. I never have to take anything twice. As
Beauty she has the naïveté, the simplicity and just that suggestion
of superiority of someone who has seen things which her family
have not even dreamt about. She dominates Ludovic, is protective
of her father, but returns to her old surroundings without the least
shame. She spoke her line: "Who has done my washing?" dressed
in pearls, tulle, silk and gold, yet even so without losing her simple
manner. After lunch I hung the sheets over the poles at the back
of the orchard. Beauty, her father, Ludovic and Avenant sit with
their backs to us facing the sheet which was lifted at the end of the
scene shot in the first location. Thus this turned-up sheet reveals
the house. Beauty kisses her father and then moves into the scene
with Avenant and Ludovic which I shot this morning. As Avenant
moves out of frame toward the right, he lets the sheet fall again.
In this way the sequence ends, as it began, with a linen curtain.
From there we went to the left-hand avenue of the orchard. From
this avenue of trees I took the shot of Beauty, who appears on the
distant house steps with her father; this causes the stupefied
Félicie, espying her over a sheet, to cry: "Look, a lady from the
Court, with my father—on his feet again."

A second shot of Beauty and her father coming toward us
through the mottled shadows of the leaves causes Avenant to
exclaim: "But it's Beauty!" I was lucky enough to have a cock crow
right in the middle of their walk. The sun moved behind the house.
We ran to meet it and, on the wing, caught the shot of Marcel
André bending down from his horse to Beauty: "And you,
Beauty, what shall I bring you?" It is this shot which leads to her
close-up reply: "Bring me a rose, father, for none grow here."
This is followed by her sisters' mocking laughter, shot yesterday.

We finished up with the shot of Beauty taken from behind
turning her head to the left (the horse goes off between her and
the house steps), because it was six o'clock, and from then on
the unions make the company pay overtime.

I decided not to shoot tomorrow, Sunday. Mila's still too ill,
which leaves me only makeshifts. If she's well enough by Monday
I will tackle the scenes of the necklace and the sedan chairs.

The crossbows are hopeless. I shall have to use longbows or

slings.

Fêtes celebrating the liberation of Tours going on all this evening and tomorrow. (Josette refuses to ride Aramis, so some girl, a neighbor of the owner of Rochecorbon, is to stand in for her.)

A bit of luck: Clément and his wife arrived this evening. I will no longer be alone in my struggle with objects, clouds, continuity and planes. I shall have the assistance and advice of the man who has just completed *La Bataille du rail* single-handed. It's a wonderful film acted entirely by railway workers and engines.

He has only the derailment left to shoot—with eleven tracking cameras. I told him that the style of my film requires modern accessories, anything that comes to hand—watering cans, benches, etc. That's the way to avoid the picturesque at all costs. The costumes are sufficient.

Sunday.

Rest. Luckily it was a fairly cloudy day. Mila's getting better. The hotel proprietor tells me that last night (fête for the liberation of Tours) Jeannot jumped fully dressed into the fountain in the town hall square. It must have been five o'clock this morning when they came in: they're all still asleep.

I know nothing quite so well-defined as the relationship between Josette and her sisters in the film, and it's exactly the same off the set. I don't mean that Mila and Nane go around nagging Josette; they are sincerely good and kind. What I mean is that these two form one distinct group in their habits and Josette another, whereas Michel, who has both reserve and exuberance, partakes of both styles. When we aren't shooting he plays the flute.

Jeannot forms another group all to himself. He gets on with the others but at the same time is aloof. He is, as it were, a friend but not a member of the family.

With these appropriate temperamental differences between the artists, it's almost unnecessary for me to tell them about the feeling of the scenes. They move and speak in the proper rhythm right away.

Michel, whom I chose after seeing his tryout for *L'Eternel Retour*[10]

[10][1943 film directed by Jean Delannoy, with screenplay and dialogue by Cocteau. Michel Auclair was not a member of the cast.]

(role of Lionel), is still paralyzed by the camera. If I restrain him he stiffens up entirely. Therefore, I let him do "a little too much" and thus run the risk of getting grimaces instead of that joyous mobility of his eyes and mouth. He'll loosen up in a few days and then I'll shoot his important scenes.

Christian Bérard's part is immensely important in making the film. It's strange having to invent some sort of formula so that we can list him in the credits without coming up against union regulations. His costumes, with their elegance, power and sumptuous simplicity, play just as big a part as the dialogue. They are not merely decorations; they reinforce the slightest gesture, and the artists find them comfortable. What a pity that France cannot yet afford the luxury of color films. The arrival of Beauty at the washhouse, wearing her grand sky-blue dress and surrounded by black chickens, was an absolute miracle.

The Paquin people must have used what materials they could find, without worrying about color. In spite of that, this fortuitous contrast of colors is dazzling and probably more exciting than if it had been deliberately chosen. As soon as Mila, Nane, Jeannot, Michel and Josette are dressed, made up and bewigged, and wander about the garden, the farm, stone-work, windows and doors come to life. In our modern clothes we all look like intruders, ridiculous ghosts.

When the light gets bad and the clouds start moving so mysteriously that the assistant cameraman, watching through his yellow glass, can no longer be sure what's going to happen, I lie down on the grass, close my eyes and let my poem (*La Crucifixion*)[11] work on me. It carries me so far away that I lose all contact with my surroundings, and when the look-out man shouts that the sun's coming out again, I look as though I am waking with a start.

Sunday, 11:30.

Undoing my dressing I noticed I have a small boil coming. R. told me that this might happen, that by going away I was preventing him from immunizing me. All I ask is that the boil

[11] [A long poem (published 1946) in which personal and universal suffering are seen in relation to the crucifixion of Christ.]

doesn't get bad before I finish shooting the exteriors.

I forgot to mention something good. Ara is paying attention to the artists and now comes onto the set. A simple little remark I made changed his attitude.

Marais just came into my room. His boil is enormous, and in a very bad place on the inside of his thigh. I have just been through all that, and I wonder what would be the best thing to do. R. has convinced me that ordinary doctors don't know how to treat this illness, and I'm not happy being at Tours so far from his advice.

Sunday, midnight.

We dined with my brother and sister-in-law at Champgault. Came home under a starry sky, in the distance a black storm with silent lightning.

Cinéma Majestic. Exciting moment. Our first projection. I've just got back from it. It's very, very beautiful. It has a robust clarity, richness of detail and poetry. Alekan has understood my style. There is relief, contour, contrasts, with something imponderable like a light wind blowing through. This emboldens me to go on working. Tomorrow, with the sun's permission, we'll tackle the necklace scene. I was on the spot with Clément and Alekan at four o'clock. We worked out the angles for the shots. I don't like making up my mind about them too far ahead. That way the film contains more fresh surprises. What's Alekan's work like? Like a piece of old silver which has been polished till it shines like new. One can find that exact sort of soft brilliance in certain pieces of silver which have been polished up with skins.

Monday morning, 7 o'clock.

Jeannot came to my room to put on his dressing. The boil is a real carbuncle and it's getting even bigger. He's going to see the doctor this evening. He will have to get an antibiotic injection. The awful thing is, he would ride a horse if necessary. He walks with some difficulty.

Escoffier and Darbon have gone to Paris. They are coming back the day after tomorrow, bringing the four lackeys and the nobleman with them.

Monday evening, 11 o'clock.

A day when the threads of fate entangled and tied themselves into knots.

Alas, Mila and Jeannot are such heroes that they'd film half-dead. Thick fog this morning. We set up the cameras behind the sheets at the back of the orchard. The mist lifted at eleven o'clock. We did the reverse-shot scene of the heads showing above the linen. Mila couldn't get down from the bench. Jeannot carried her. I added a line: "You leave me alone" as if he were helping her out of scorn. Camera and lamps were moved. I prepared the meeting scene with the necklace. I tackled it after a thousand and one difficulties, since Alekan, with the inhumanity of all cameramen, mathematicians and astronomers, was arranging and correcting his lights without realizing that Mila could hardly stand on her feet.

Lunch. Clouds came. Rain. I went to sleep after lunch. I opened an eye. I guessed that the unit was playing "portraits"[12] in the little laundry where I was lying. The sun was shining. I got up. The actors had taken their make-up off and changed. I questioned Clément. He told me that the set-builders wouldn't work after four o'clock unless they got overtime according to their union rates. Darbon has refused these terms on principle. He's in Paris. Clément argued, took it upon himself and us to pay the overtime, and got things moving again. The cameras and lights were put in place. We made up the actors, did their hair and dressed them.

The sun was sinking, so that Alekan had to change his angle. Then began the torture of watching Mila, who is very, very ill but is trying to make light of things, for, at all costs, she wants to avoid having a lawsuit with the other company she's filming for. She wants to leave tomorrow evening and come back Saturday.

I suspect she's worse than she shows and even worse than she imagines. No doubt her journey will crack her up completely so that she won't be able to do her film in Paris, or get back here— which will mutilate ours.

All this proved too much for her; she broke down under the fatigue, pain and nervous tension, stammering, swaying, her face contorted. She was on the verge of hysterics. The second shot (which would have saved us) missed fire. The clear sky clouded

---

[12][A word game for several players, similar to "Botticelli."]

over again. Only a few minutes were left. The nerve storm broke. Mila collapsed on her knees, sobbing, among the lettuces. She was carried off.

I went with Jeannot to Tours to see Dr. Vial. He had us wait in a bar there where we were given white wine and *rillettes*[13] on bread. He took us to his clinic on the road to Rochecorbon. He gave Marais a local anesthetic, then lanced the carbuncle on his leg. Jeannot is very tough and brave, but seemed to be suffering terribly. I left him at the clinic. Tomorrow morning we will pick him up on our way. I'll avoid doing the scenes with the horse and will shoot something quiet. The doctor is going to make him lie still for twenty-four hours, by which time the carbuncle should be ripe.

Imagine the problems of a disastrous undertaking, where the sun is our boss, and we have to arrange the scenes so Marcel André can finish and our invalids won't be overtaxed.

Tuesday evening, 11 o'clock.

A good day, a run of luck. Mist lifted; sun in a blue sky, with clouds covering and uncovering it. Fairly quick shots; the horse doing exactly what it was supposed to do. The scenes were exactly as I visualized them. Mila held out. Jeannot, who had slept at the clinic, managed to film, then returned there in his LeNain[14] costume for another lancing.

By six o'clock this evening I had taken eleven shots and had finished with Marcel. Even the necklace scene is in the can.

Madame T., Mila's agent, arrived at the hotel with an ambulance to take her to Paris, so that she can fulfill her engagements there. She's quite mad, for Mila is luckily insured in both films, and runs no risk of financial collapse. The insurance company's doctor came to the hotel. It was Vial. He was worried. She'll have to be X-rayed tomorrow morning. If there is the smallest crack in her pelvis she'll have to go into plaster and our film will collapse.

Jeannot won't be able to ride for a week. I will be brave and accept the impossible. Whatever happens I shall nurse them and get on with the film. I will add this *tour de force* to a thousand others. I go to bed utterly exhausted, and so thin that a woman journalist

---

[13][A type of minced pork, a speciality of Touraine celebrated by Rabelais and Balzac among others.]
[14][The seventeenth-century brothers LeNain–Antoine, Louis and Mathieu–specialized in genre paintings, including many showing peasant families.]

declares: "His face is made of his two profiles stuck together."

Notes taken on the spot. Wednesday morning,
September 5, 1945, 11 o'clock.

I'll snatch this story out of nothingness, by surprise tactics. And if fate's against me I'll deal with fate. I'll cheat it with some card trick.

I live in another world, a world where time and place are wholly mine. I live there without newspapers, letters, telegrams, telephone, without any contact with the outside world.

The mist lifted this morning but the clouds crossed, then superimposed themselves in every direction. We had to take the shot of the horse ridden by the local girl who is standing in for Josette. I did it "silent" so that I could shout my orders. Clément was hidden in the barn pouring tetrachloride on Aramis's hooves and false tail.

Workmen, hidden behind beams and firewood, held the invisible string which opened the yard gates. A two-yard-high scaffolding dominated the scene. A crack of the whip, and Aramis appeared. I gave the orders for the gates to open. They opened. Aramis hesitated, then pranced out like a dancer. We speeded up the camera so as to slow down his movements on the screen. Three blue rents in the sky gave us enough time to get this shot in the can.

The car brought Marais back from the clinic where Mila was being X-rayed. Our next shot was to be the one where he (Marais) fetches the horse from the courtyard and leads it into the barn by the bridle.

The weather broke up. A black cumulus drifted toward the half-light of the sun, whose disc was pale as the moon. I was writing outdoors on a table opposite sheds stuffed full of the possessions of LeNain's peasants. I was cold so they brought me the Merchant's enormous dressing-gown.

Cameras and spotlights emigrated toward the farmyard. The girl standing in for Josette dismounted in the midst of her escorting family. They are an astonishing collection and remind one of Caran d'Ache's[15] horsemen. Marais limps. The workmen are

---

[15] [Pseudonym (from the Russian word for "pencil") of Emmanuel Poiré (1859–1909), famous illustrator and cartoonist who specialized in military and equestrian subjects.]

Avenant leads Magnificent (Aramis) out of the stable (pp. 25, 93ff.).
This scene was shot partly at Rochecorbon, partly at Saint-Maurice.

Hammond Collection

A Rochecorbon exterior. In her flight, Beauty touches the iron ring
with the monster's head (p. 25).

buying and reselling brandy. Clément, who has just come from Brittany, is beginning to understand the caprices of this sky which can cloud over and clear again in the space of five minutes.

Midday.

At the moment we are sitting in the straw and oats. The camera tracks divide the barn in two in the direction of the big plank door. We are keeping one eye on the sun. Marais has already rehearsed. The difficulties he finds in turning Aramis will fill the frame superbly. Before the door opens I add the line for him: "*I am going,*" to explain why he walks so resolutely. The real reason is that it is easier for him to stride than to amble. He is in pain when he hesitates.

As I write these lines Marais asks us if he should stay or go to the clinic. Clément reports two layers of cloud. I give the order to lunch. We shall see later. Stop.

1 o'clock.

We have lunched. Everything upsets my diet. The owner gave me oysters. I'll have the tracking rails put up in front of the house in the corner of the courtyard. I'll take Beauty's flight by moonlight. She'll wear her cape and walk the whole length of the house, till she reaches the iron ring decorated with the head of a horned monster. Then she'll look to the right and to the left. Alekan will close-up on Beauty and this beast which, in her father's home, gave a preview of her future. This seventeenth-century ironwork impressed me the very first day I discovered the house. It was *the* house.

The car brought news of Mila. No bones broken. A month's rest. I've been told I can use her tomorrow. That gives me tomorrow and the next day. The "little lackeys" are at Tours. If we get any sun I'll be able to finish with Mila and then she can rest.

Beauty's exit by moonlight—a fatal shot. (Had to use a red filter.) Alekan just got his lamps, screens and rails fixed, then the sun had to move. Now shadows spoiled everything. I told him so. But how can you talk to a cameraman, even a charming one, who opposes you with all the indifference of the stars?

Finally, Alekan declared that he had nothing left but shadow.

It was now four o'clock. Marais hadn't come back from the clinic yet. I decided to try the close-up "Bring me a rose." We set it up. Marais arrived. He was limping horribly. After an interminable delay I gave the order to shoot. Josette did the second take marvelously. But "sound" told me that a plane drowned the last phrase. Josette was nervous and tense and couldn't recapture her relaxed simplicity. Now she was either too simple or not simple enough. I persisted and only stopped after the seventh take. But I was worried. So I decided to take one more. I took two. (Nine takes in all.) The sound people always exaggerate. Probably it is the bad take that will turn out to be the best.

Marais, exhausted by his pain, was in a very bad temper. He went back to the clinic. He's to be operated on tomorrow morning, which means we won't have him for two days. I'll take the opportunity and use Mila in the scene of the departure by sedan chair.

I "broke down" the sedan chair with Clément and Alekan and arranged the set so that Mila need move as little as possible.

I wonder. I ask myself whether or not these exhausting days may not be the sweetest of my life. For they are filled with friendship, harmless quarrels, laughter and contain moments when we seem to hold fleeting time in our hands.

Thursday the 6th, 7 p.m.

Overcast. The insurance company will pay up for Mila and Jeannot. They're living at the clinic. Here at Rochecorbon everybody was freezing and trying to keep warm under a pile of costumes. Escoffier dressed the little lackeys. I rehearsed them in the farmyard. We decided to try the two shots which can be lit artificially. I shot Nane waking Blin's brother, who was asleep in a cart full of straw. We lunched by the heat of a thousand-watt lamp and ended up by believing it was the sun. Aldo went quite mad and took innumerable photos at the table with us, some of the lackeys and some of the actresses who were sprawling in the straw. Darbon came from the clinic. They had left Mila there as the weather was so dull. Jeannot had had his operation. Alekan decided to shoot the short scene which takes place at the wash-house without waiting for the sun. So the car went off to fetch Mila. We mussed up her and Nane at the last minute, throwing skirts and men's shirts on them. We tied some kind of rag round their hair. I didn't think much of this scene at first, but now it's become very lovely. These fair-skinned girls surrounded by the disordered sheets, the frothing lather, Mila's burst of laughter, Nane seizing a bundle of linen and throwing it at the camera—all this excitement makes me think of the *Armance* wash-house and the hunchback doctor.* Unfortunately, there was nothing else I could do. The laundry was now a melee of lackeys, make-up men and dressers. They were all singing Russian songs in unison. Mila tried on her grand party dress. I left. I went to the clinic. The car dropped me at the bottom of the hill. Moulouk was off like an arrow. I found him waiting outside Jeannot's door. Mila and Michel came and joined us. Gradually the whole company installed itself in this model clinic. I'm thinking of spending several days here to start the insulin treatment again.

If it's sunny tomorrow, I hope to shoot the sedan chair scene with the little lackeys. And with a bit of luck that will leave Mila free.

Why is the theme of "actors at a resting place" or "actors on a journey" so compelling? The sight of theater wings in the open air is surprising. I never tire of it. It makes up for the endless waiting. Nothing could describe the pleasant atmosphere of our hotel (Hôtel de Bordeaux) in spite of its lack of comfort. It's like being at boarding school, or on vacation, or traveling. Living together, working and discussing the work; that, to me, represents the height of luxury.

Friday the 7th, 5 a.m.

I saw a short projection last night. Jeannot chopping wood. Michel filling the watering cans. The sisters on the house steps with their father. It's irritating to see so little. I'll wait for a proper run-through. But I'm well aware of the difficulty presented by a film in which every shot contains only a short sentence or a few lines. The rhythm is produced only by the entire film, and the actors can't understand what they are doing. It's my job to follow this thread which escapes them and keep them on the right path. That's what makes film acting so difficult. If the actor hasn't absolute confidence in the director he always imagines that his lines are unimportant, and consequently tends to speak them without conviction, with the result that the whole film is weak.

* I cut this shot in the editing. It was going on too long.

Another difficulty lies in trying to find a style that is true without being realistic, which stays in relation to the costumes and the strangeness of the story. I must remember not to let them talk too loudly, but at the same time make them see the importance of the words.

A starry sky, but that doesn't mean anything, for we often have fine nights only to find cloud in the morning.

Friday midnight.

Very hot day. Sunshine. We had to take Mila's shots. She might not be strong enough tomorrow. We were in the farmyard, chairs all ready. The animals, locked in, passed by in all directions. Mila, with dark blue dress and felt hat, was arrogantly smart.

I shot the scene in which the sisters arrive, furious at finding the lackey asleep in the chair. The shot of Mila getting into her chair and settling herself as if she's on the lavatory. The shot of her shouting through the door.

I had lunch with the L's,[16] while the chair-carrying scene was being prepared. We were bothered by cloud. After lunch I just managed to snatch the shot of Ludovic shutting his sisters into the chairs and their moving off. Another shot of the chairs being carried. The lackey kicking the cellar door. The chairs were heavy. Paul, dressed as a lackey, dropped the handles twice running. If this takes all right, I'll cut to a close-up of Nane crying: "They've been drinking!"

A tracking shot following Mila in close-up. I wanted to take a close-up of Nane but she was ill. The sun was faint, she was fainting. We stopped.

I went to the clinic. Jeannot is better. I went back to the hotel. I slept like a log. I woke up at ten o'clock. I found the others downstairs. I dined. Projection at the Majestic at eleven o'clock.

Here's our reward—the run-through was wonderful. Sparkling, soft and clear. Alekan had got just what I wanted. I was delighted. I saw just what I had imagined. First special effect: the necklace. Camera angle. The false necklace falls out of sight, the real one into sight, and thus it looks as though it's changed in its fall.

---

[16] [The Lecours, owners of the Rochecorbon property.]

A Rochecorbon exterior. A lackey asleep in a sedan chair (p. 28).

Cocteau preparing an exterior shot at Rochecorbon.

Saturday the 8th, midnight.

Have just got back from the Majestic, where I showed Lebreton yesterday's run-through.

Spent the day waiting for the sun. The morning mist turned into innumerable little clouds, all joined together by a veil. Clément and I prepared some shots which need the sun, and some others we had up our sleeve which don't. At midday, the sun came out. Then a mad race began of actors, make-up men and set-builders, and a chase after fowls and goats. We shot the departure of the sedan chairs, using Mila's stand-in. We took the shot of Nane opening the door of her chair to find it full of chickens. The chickens squawked and refused to stay in the chair. So the workmen had to get busy putting the fowls to sleep by catching them, stuffing their heads under their wings and whirling them around at arm's length. The chickens went to sleep. Then we put them back in the chair. I gave the order to shoot. Nane came forward, spoke her line, opened the door, and cried out. The chickens flew out, one through the door, the others through the windows of the chair. Then Nane settled herself inside and sat down on a hen, saying: "These chairs are filthy." At that moment two ducks came out in single file from beneath her skirts. I was terrified that someone might burst out laughing, but we controlled ourselves and took the shot.

Lunch. We shot the scene of the little lackeys waking up. After that, the close-ups of Nane which will be used for intercutting in the scene of the departure in the sedan chairs (the one where the chair wobbles and is dropped by one of the lackeys). She cries out: "They've been drinking!" after which the chair is righted and the procession starts off again. Thanks to this shot, I will try to use the ones I spoilt, which may be curious.*

M. came all the way from Paris to get a wet sheet thrown in his face. That's just like film work. Clément threw it at him from behind the camera. It is, of course, supposed to be the same sheet that Nane throws, in the wash-house scene. In that way I can show the cloth flying toward the audience, and arriving full in the draper's face. Then we set up the shot of Nane at the window. The sun disappeared. We packed up.

Clinic. Jeannot will probably be able to work again on Tuesday. Mila is more comfortable. Aldo took the opportunity to have an immediate operation on cysts on his face. He returned along with

* Which I did.

us masked with gauze and sticking-plaster.

The doctor told me that if Marais has a special dressing he can do the horse scene the day after tomorrow. I shall take the opportunity to retake the shot where he first sees Magnificent. The shot's too short and taken from too far away, missing the expression on his face.

First big write-up on our work in the *Monde Illustré*. Photograph of me, during our preparation, on the cover. Looks like a sad old man gazing into the distance. This is me. I must get used to it. I get so lost in my work that I forget that I exist and change. Suddenly I find myself face to face with a person I didn't know, but that my friends do. We're to lunch at my brother's on Sunday.

I suppose the reason why Christian Bérard can go about dressed in rags, and I can go about looking shaggy and wearing a dirty old hat far too small for me, is that we become so absorbed in the spectacle every minute offers that we think we are invisible and that others can no more see us than we can see ourselves. Unfortunately, photographers teach us the truth, but they don't cure us of thinking that we look as we think we do.

The uglier the years make us, the more beautiful our works should become, reflecting us like a child who looks like us.

Sunday the 9th, 11 a.m.

The cloudy weather is consolation for a "free" day—which is just imprisonment for me. I can never do too much. Work never exhausts me. It's afterwards that I fall into the black pit.

Thinking of what I've done so far—it's not so bad. No doubt the editing can cover up my mistakes and my lack of interest in perfect continuity (which worries Lucienne, my continuity girl, to death). Take too much care, leave no doors open to chance, and poetry, which is difficult enough to trap, will be frightened away. A little improvisation tames it. Trees where there will be none, something where it shouldn't be, such as a hat off a head in one shot but on again in the next, are as it were, cracks in the wall through which poetry can penetrate. Those who notice such spelling mistakes don't really know how to read and are not enchanted by the story. No matter.

Yesterday in the sedan-chair scene I used a long tracking shot.

Finally, I deleted it. This film must prove that it's possible to avoid camera movement and keep to a fixed frame.

A day late in our schedule. We've taken about forty shots. The owners of Rochecorbon get 80,000 francs for two weeks. After which time they get 5,000 francs a day. That's nothing to worry about, because the insurance on our invalids will cover the excess. A wet day costs us 100,000 francs.

Sunday evening.

Lunched at my brother's with Josette, Nane, Michel and the doctor. Bathed in the river. Raspberries.

Monday the 10th, midnight.

This morning we took the opening shot of the film: the target and arrows. We recorded the sound of the arrows. As always the real sound was false. We had to translate it, invent a sound more exact than the sound itself. Clément found the solution by whipping the air with a thin switch. The sun wouldn't oblige. I said: "I'm going to the clinic. As soon as my back is turned the sun will come out." At the clinic, sunshine. I found the shot had been taken when I got back. We prepared the scene of Jeannot and Josette for tomorrow. We shot Nane at the window and started again on Josette's flight by moonlight. I had her lips made up very dark because of the red filter. The dog that belongs to the manor refused to film. He took up his place all right but left it as soon as the scene began, then lay down again afterwards. Sumptuous lunch at the manor. Restless sleep. I dozed off in the laundry on the flea-ridden bed. Clément woke me up. I had been dreaming and jumped with both feet into a reality that is no more real than my dream: the end of Josette's course, up to the door of the barn. The airplanes went mad. Superfortresses flew over us. I had to take the scene silent, the sound to be added afterwards. Through with Nane. She's leaving tomorrow. I shall use a stand-in to show her back at the edge of the frame in the shot taken from the room. We gave the unit a holiday for we couldn't go on without Jeannot. It was five o'clock. I went back to the clinic, where Mila gave us tea. Michel, clad in a white smock, had been watching Dr. Vial's operations ever since eight o'clock this morning. He described them. I felt uneasy giddiness in my legs and stomach. I escaped. I lay down at the hotel, overcome with extraordinary tiredness. Exhausted by Touraine and the break in the rhythm of our work. The whole unit woke me at eight o'clock and took me off to eat at a bistrot.

Tuesday the 11th, 7 a.m.

I must see if I can put the scene of the sisters in the room (they're dressing) in the place of the tavern scene and the tavern after the scene with the sisters. That would allow me to cut from Mila's head after the shot where I cut from Josette's head out of frame, then bring Mila back into the frame, wearing her high-heaped wig just when she is finishing tying the ribbons. (Another advantage will be that I won't have shots of Avenant and Ludovic following one another.)

Clément is amazed by the amiable way our unit works together. He has just come from a very tough and unpleasant world. He's leaving us for three days. He has to shoot the derailment of the armored train in Brittany. Weather permitting, the derailment is set for Thursday. We were all to go there, but I shall be too busy at Epinay and seeing to Jeannot's make-up as the Beast, which I find less terrifying than I did at the first test.

I can't praise enough the workmen and electricians who are working with us. It's marvelous watching them work so quickly and without a suggestion of bad temper. They really contribute to the film. They like it. They understand it and think of a thousand and one ways to please me.

There's no barrier between them and the actors. They each look after their own affairs and in that way make up a unit.

I have been thinking of what we've done so far here in Touraine. I must avoid a certain kind of coldness which results from the way I work and might be dangerous. It was possible to treat the film in an entirely different way, and show the girls doing the washing, pushing each other and bustling about. Instinctively I am after a very simple line and gags of a visual order—Jeannot lifting the sheet back, the heads appearing, the necklace falling . . . . The other method wouldn't suit the short lines that I have given the characters. These lines, as well as the costumes, call for effects stripped of complicated gesticulation and clutter. It is worth noticing that, apart from Beauty when she's dressed as a princess, none of the women wear jewelry.

In the rest of the film (to be done at the studio) I will supply the movement and detail—but I suspect that the rhythm of the film resides in me more than in the mobility of the camera or of the protagonists. Perhaps I won't be able to do very much in the face of a mechanism which will only come to realization in the cutting-room. The main thing is to add one fact to another, to interest the spectator instead of distracting him.

Tried to make Aramis rear with two people on his back. He refused. I'm not happy about his dancing gait. Like some actresses, he will have to be photographed only from certain angles. I must avoid his legs (except when he's galloping). I must frame his powerful neck, like those of the horses of Marly,[17] and his head in profile, with its fine veins and big eye.

I am writing this, this morning, while waiting for the car. We're not leaving till nine o'clock. The new time is upsetting for us. At ten o'clock it's eight by the sun. At six o'clock in the evening it is only four and thus the unit misses two excellent hours.

The doctor is letting Jeannot film quiet scenes today, and tomorrow, with a special dressing, we'll do him leaving the farm on Aramis.

If it's overcast this morning I shall try to squeeze in the shot with the longbows and do the retake of Avenant when he sees the horse enter the courtyard.

Last month, coming out of the Rue d'Athènes, where they were showing *Le Sang d'un Poète*,[18] I told Gide that I couldn't bear to see the film again because each shot is so slow. He replied that I was wrong, that this slowness was a rhythm, and that these slow shots coming one after another formed a special tempo, my tempo, a procedure of my own.

No doubt he's right, and it would be dangerous to upset a rhythm that comes from within oneself, through fear of this rhythm, and to impose another, artificial, one which would not suit it. (I must sleep *a little*.)

[17] [A pair of statues of spirited Numidian horses with men standing beside them, executed by the sculptor Guillaume (1er) Coustou between 1740 and 1745 for the royal château at Marly. In 1794 the painter David had them moved to the Place de la Concorde in Paris (flanking the entrance to the Champs-Elysées), where they are today.]

[18] [Made in 1930, this was the only film Cocteau had directed himself before *Beauty and the Beast*.]

Wednesday the 12th, 8 a.m.

I was too tired to write last night. It was the day of the archery, the Josette and Jeannot scene, the Jeannot–Michel–draper passage which comes before the Italian farce scene. I shot them the way I wanted with intervals of luck, waiting, strained nerves, shattered nerves, and planes passing.

The sky, very gloomy in the morning, cleared about eleven (nine by the sun). The archery scene is exactly as I visualized it when I wrote the film at the Palais-Royal. The film will start with successive close-ups: the target, the arrow hitting it, the backs of Avenant and Ludovic, the arrow landing in the room and frightening the dog. I've added a big close-up of Jeannot's hands drawing the bow just as Michel knocks into him. The arrow flies off. I faked the whistling of it by swishing a stick near the microphone.

A shot through the window. We disguised the dresser to double for Nane where she appears at the edge of the frame. But Nane, with her usual sweetness, came and offered to get dressed and do the shot herself.

After a shot of Jeannot and Michel entering the house, the unit had lunch.

The previous evening, in case of bad light, we had prepared the shot of the Josette–Jeannot scene behind the house, and had rigged up a tarpaulin and placed the scaffolding on the road so that we could have the spotlights on the top of the wall. This take was long and painful (till six o'clock). Whenever Jeannot had got into the scene and was acting with great intensity, some technical fault, or a plane, would interrupt him. Finally we got two very good takes, and I'll have the bad ones printed just in case they are any use. The miracle of machines must be kept in mind. At eight, we shot the scene that precedes the farce sequence. Perfect style. Goldoni, Molière. Alekan lit it without the sun, as though it were just setting and throwing long shadows.

Dr. Vial came to watch us work. Cloudless sky this morning. I wouldn't be surprised if, now that we're leaving, they don't get a whole week of lovely weather, just to spite us. Departure set for tomorrow.

Wednesday, 7 o'clock.

I have just checked the time by the watch that Marais brought me from Switzerland. It's a hundred-lire coin. You press your nail on the edge opposite the D of Italy [*sic*] and the coin opens and out comes the flattest watch in the world. Seven o'clock. Nothing more of our gypsy camp remains at Rochecorbon. I was sorry to leave. I had got used to living there and inventing life there. A golden wine flowed there as from a spring. The workmen drank an incredible number of bottles. Aldo kept trying to get me into a corner. He'd got hold of a very rare old bottle and wanted to share it with me. Our last work here was done under a radiant sky without a single cloud. Looking back, bless the clouds we've had, for they are the peculiar glory of the Touraine sky. And even when the sun avoids them, they give the light the elegance of pearl. Without them everything would have been too raw. Too raw and too easy. Every shot has been a struggle but I dare to say that I have done what I set out to do. Not a single shot has left me miserable at a gap between what is and what should have been. If there are faults, they are mine and I can't blame anybody else.

First shot of the day was at eleven o'clock: Jeannot and Michel leaving the barn on Aramis. He reared today, which he refused to do yesterday. The camera got it.

The third time the horse came out of the barn it suddenly started to back in again, shaking Michel off, and reappeared without him. Last shot. Midday. Avenant, with Ludovic up behind him, is supposed to gallop toward us and then go off to the left after brushing against the camera. That's when the trouble began. Aramis kicked or bolted. Michel, clinging madly to Jeannot, without saddle or stirrup, risked breaking his own neck and aroused laughter. He tried again but his acrobatics became so serious (Jeannot was riding with his wound open) that I told them to stop. We'll have to use stand-ins.

One o'clock. I prepared the shot where Avenant and Ludovic join the sisters in the barn before the horse comes in.

Third shot. A close-up of Avenant sticking his head out of the barn when he sees Magnificent arrive. Lunch. After lunch we shot the scene we'd set up at one o'clock. I shot the gallop at three o'clock. The stable boy wore Avenant's clothes. Lucile (the continuity girl) doubled for Ludovic. Aramis, without Michel's weight up, was better, but still didn't like two riders. He was up to his tricks. At last he galloped and with that speed and all that movement, I'm sure that no one will notice the subterfuge.

But Marais is not happy about it. In *Carmen,*[19] he wouldn't let a double go on, and insisted on playing the most dangerous scenes. As in the war, so in film-work, his courage is the outcome of the astonishing conviction that he cannot come to any harm. But I am working from a different theory. In films a trick shot is better than the real thing. It heightens the scene. The actuality seems tame. I am speaking about daredevil scenes. For these an acrobat is better than an actor.

4 o'clock.

Only recordings—the switch whipping the air and imitating the arrow; Beauty calling the Beast. (Josette stumbling over a ploughed field. It looked as though she were running around a M. Loyal,[20] who was, in fact, none other than Bouboule armed with a pole. Some local women were peeping over a distant hedge, following this strange sight through their opera glasses.) That's the lot here. We kissed. We celebrated. Aldo took a photograph of the unit. We packed. We didn't look back. I got into the car. I left.

I drove up that lovely hill which I had come down with Maurette and Moulaert the day I first discovered the manor. I was then panicky at the thought that I might not get permission to film there. I visited other places just in case . . . but now my job there is done. The way time solves things is an enigma.

I said to Michel yesterday: "God uses up centuries in an incredible fashion." As we do minutes.

What I've got to do now at Joinville is to turn that past into the present. But it will never be the Lecours' house again, it will always be the one in the fairy tale.

Thursday the 13th.

We drove off at nine o'clock. Stopped at the Saint-Grégoire clinic to pick up Marais. Said goodbye to Mila, who was to spend another week there. A ridiculously small bill, thanks to Dr. Vial's generosity.

Being superstitious, I insisted on stopping at the inn where we

---

[19] [The one directed by Christian-Jaque, with Viviane Romance in the title role and Marais as Don José (1944).]

[20] [A term for the man who introduces comic and equestrian numbers in circus performances.]

drank some Vouvray when we first came to Tours. We drank to the success of the film and then continued on to Barbizon, where I wanted to show Emile the road with fairyland trees which Poligny had brought me to see for *Baron Fantôme*.

I was riding with Josette, Jeannot, Darbon and Moulouk. The windows were wide open. A soft blue air whipped our faces. Darbon apparently likes the troupe and the film. I have an idea for the credits. I'll use clapper boards (the black board we use to show the number of the take). I'll have one of the men show the boards, clap at the names of the stars and then just show them for a second, as if they were going to film. We had lunch at Barbizon, at the Charmettes. We got very little to eat for 4,000 francs [*sic*]. Then I looked for the road with the dead trees, but couldn't find it. I gave up.

We got back to Paris. Palais-Royal. Mountains of letters. Sleep. Tomorrow I shall go to Epinay, where Moulaert should have got the undergrowth cleared and installed my set.

Friday the 14th, 8:30 p.m.

Been to Epinay, where three productions have to be done together; this will ration our electric current. The noise of trains and planes hinders our work. All the scenes of the sick Beast by the lake will have to be shot at night.

This lake is in reality a stinking stream draining the sewers. But, like a dog, once I've found a place, I get attached to it, and this mundane setting will suit the anti-pompous style which I am trying to recapture, the style of *Le Sang d'un Poète*. The forest gate was placed badly. Tried, with Darbon, Alekan and Moulaert, to find the right place, getting drenched by rain among the nettles. After endless obstacles (shots that never matched up with the reverse shots), I discovered the right place, and Alekan marked out where his platforms will have to be fixed. It's a nuisance to make Josette and Jeannot act in this bog. But I'm convinced that Bérard was right when he said that the scenes will be more moving beside this dirty water and among these weeds than it would be in a luxurious setting.

At 6:30 I went back to Paulvé's house. Claude Ibéria, who has recovered, was waiting for us there. Projection. The room in Paulvé's house distorts the sound and the image. But in spite of these yellow and nasal rushes I could tell that the scene with the sedan chairs has come off. (Some shots are still missing. The best ones, naturally.)

Aldo brought me some excellent stills this morning.When I got back to the Palais-Royal at eight o'clock, he gave me some more. I'll sort them all out this evening.

Saturday evening, 11 o'clock.

I went with Alekan and Aldo to have a look round Raray. We got to Senlis at nine o'clock. Every time I see Raray it's a new discovery. Aldo was absolutely bowled over. I made him take as many photographs as he could, so that he can work on the sets. We were so sorry that we couldn't shoot on the spot that we decided to try to persuade the firm to let us do that. We had lunch at Senlis. We went to Epinay. Not enough workmen, cables or lights. A dreary stinking barn of a place. The workmen were putting up the gate. Darbon arrived. We told him that it would be crazy to fix the platform and all the gear of a studio round such worthless décor. Far better build the set in the studio.We would agree to shoot the gate at Epinay, and would go to Raray for two days, where Alekan proposes to shoot even in grey weather, with very little electricity. Darbon consented. He will postpone our starting again till next week.

At Paulvé's, I showed Claude what I brought back from Rochecorbon. The lab is getting the rushes all muddled up. Some shots are missing, others aren't synchronized. She's going to check the negative on Monday, and will prepare a proper projection at which I can choose the takes.

With this postponement I have come to realize that the rhythm of the film is one of narrative. I am telling the story. It is as if I were hidden behind the screen, saying: "Then such and such a thing happened." The characters don't seem to be living a life of their own, but a life that is being narrated. Perhaps that's how it should be in a fairy tale.

Sunday the 16th, 7 p.m.

Conference at Paulvé's house with Alekan, Moulaert and myself. Ran through the shots we took at Raray again. Decision on the heights of the platforms and on Josette's dresses. If the light isn't too good, I'll shoot in a sort of twilight and change the time of Josette's meals. If it's sunny I'll shoot it as moonlight. Alekan suggests using the red powder which, with a sort of mobile magnesium flare, makes it possible to shoot at night. I'll take Marcel André along to do the bit where he shouts: "Hullo, is anybody there?" which is answered by the echo.

Tuesday the 18th.

Awful night. These days doing nothing leave me in a sort of vacuum. Nothing but troublesome sessions with the doctor and the barber. I sleep badly. The film unwinds in my head. I edit it, move around the lines, add some, delete others. And do all that without the material, because my editor is trying to put it in order, and she must get hold of takes which I haven't seen.

The actors phone me. They're at a loose end too. Clément has shot his derailment in Brittany. He'll be back Wednesday. I think I'll cut out the scene of the sedan chairs arriving at the Duchess's house. The sisters' return will be enough. It would have slowed up the action too much. I phoned and told Emile this good news for the firm. One exterior less certainly is something.

Tuesday evening, 11 o'clock.

I spent the day at Paulvé's editing with Claude and Lucile, who are putting the notes in order and disentangling the incredible mix-up that was made of our work when it was printed.

At B.'s this evening, Castillo spoke to me about Josette's négligé. A very difficult costume. It must be timeless, it musn't be Greek, and must lie like the dresses. I am looking for something very grand, yet very simple; very shaped, yet very free. It mustn't look like a dress, yet has to be one.

Wednesday the 19th, 11 p.m.

Disjointed day. Bérard, just back from London, lunched at the house. After lunch Emile Darbon, Claude Ibéria and Clément came to pick me up in the car and we drove out to Joinville. At Saint-Maurice, chaos began. The projection over, we visited the

stage where the workmen were building the Beast's stables.
Bérard was infuriated by the clumsy way his sketches had been
realized. He talked and talked, drew, corrected. Soon everything
was turned upside down and transformed by his fantastic talent.

I showed him the incomplete sequence of the sheets in the little
projection room which was free. (Bad projection, everything
vibrating and yellow.) He thought my camera angles were too
conventional. Perhaps that's because he doesn't realize that this
sequence doesn't open the film but follows bizarre sequences at
the Beast's castle. I needed this calmness. While waiting for the
promised reel, we talked to Renée Saint-Cyr and to Claude
Dauphin, costumed and made up as Cyrano.[21]

Marais saw only two mediocre shots. He had to go off and see the
doctor. After he left, at 6:30, the big room emptied out. The reel
was passed on to us there. Marais's mediocre scene was excellent
there. I got home at eight o'clock and dined alone. I shall see all the
rushes on Friday with Ibéria, and I'll choose the best. She'll then
start editing. We go to Senlis on Sunday. The workmen are to leave
Paris with all the gear tomorrow.

Thursday the 20th, 8 a.m.

My desire to keep the camera fixed and the shots simple makes
Bérard say my angles are flat. It's true, but I imagine that in the
editing, when passages are overlapped and intercut with unusual
studio shots, these Touraine exteriors will become meaningful.
But it certainly would be better if Alekan had an assistant and did
not have to do all the lighting and actual shooting himself—in
short, if he were free to choose the angles instead of being literally
held to a method. A mere nothing, a hair distinguishes a Vermeer
composition from those of his contemporaries.

Thursday evening, 11 o'clock.

The doctor's diagnosis of Jeannot isn't too good. It's very
worrying, seeing him look so tired, playing the Beast with all
that heavy make-up of hair and glue. But he never complains.

---

[21][Renée Saint-Cyr is an actress. The film version of *Cyrano de Bergerac* with Dauphin (1946) was
directed by Ferdinand Rivers.]

I remember his going on in *Les Parents Terribles*[22] with acute otitis. Blood spurted from his nostrils. The audience in the front row threw handkerchiefs up to him. Worrying about the invalids spoils my pleasure in the work. Mila will be leaving the clinic at Tours this week. Nane has to have another operation on her stomach as soon as the film is finished. As for me . . . .

Packed up this afternoon ready to go to Senlis. Smoke machines, red powder, magnesium torches, a thousand details which my obsession with the mechanism already set in motion may make me forget. An enormous number of people are concerned with a film, and the feeling of responsibility becomes visible, implacable, and forces a director to overcome his doubts and weaknesses. The slightest sign of discouragement would demoralize his unit. I suppose that's why, in the long run, film directors, knowing that they must appear sure of themselves, become so self-confident. Can't get hold of a stag or a doe. At last I hope to have all the work we did in Touraine by Saturday. I will then choose the shots with Ibéria and Clément.

Bérard is going to supervise the décor at Joinville.

Friday the 21st, evening.

Spent the day running between the company's office and Clément's flat, deciding the angle of the Raray shots and settling the problem of the special effects in the final scene.

The bizarre angles at Raray force themselves on you. There is the Beast, and there is Raray, the strangest park in France. For the trick shots, we have decided to truck the camera forwards and backwards on a slope, cut to a profile shot, and do the whole thing with a back projection of rolling clouds. Clément and Alekan are to go up in an English plane the day after tomorrow and shoot the clouds and the receding earth. To get the shot of the earth falling away, they'll have to do a stiff upward "dive."

Saturday the 22nd, 7 o'clock.

This morning, saw Paulvé, who seemed delighted and spoke to

[22][Marais created the role of Michel in this 1938 play by Cocteau; the role of his father Georges was created by Marcel André, the Merchant of *Beauty and the Beast*. Cocteau filmed *Les Parents Terribles* (with Marais, André and Josette Day, and with Bérard as art director) in 1948.]

me about another film next year with the same unit. Shut myself up in the projection room choosing the takes with Ibéria, Clément and Alekan. Still can't find the one of the horse rearing, and there's no trace of it on the labels. Ibéria's assistant is going to Saint-Maurice on Monday morning to hunt through the footage there. Awful if this fine shot were lost. We had lunch near the office, and afterwards met Bérard, who's just come back from Saint-Maurice. He didn't seem pleased with the way his décor's being handled. It's a pity that Moulaert has to work on two films at once. Ours requires a great deal of work. A tooth is giving me great pain. I saw a run-through of the derailment in Brittany. Twelve takes, four of which are of a tragic intensity. Immediately afterwards I ran off to a dentist, who told me I've got an abscess coming. He opened up the tooth and told me how to treat it. Now I've a rash on my fingers and my cheeks are inflamed. "To make bad blood, to make spleen," all that is true. I'm paying now for five years of bad blood and spleen. Jeannot has the same kind of rash on his hip.

It's raining. Tomorrow afternoon we leave for Senlis.

Sunday evening the 23rd, 8 o'clock.

Left Paris for Senlis at 5:30 with Josette, Jeannot and Emile Darbon. Something fell out of the car as we were going along. It was the carburetor. Hunted for it. Eventually found it and started again.

Darbon informed us that we shall be living in an abandoned château. Out of prudence, I stopped at the Grand Cerf, and found some very mediocre rooms there. We left the suitcases there and went on to Raray under an equinoctial sky cluttered with castles of slate, lakes of sulphur and pink forests. The walls of Raray looked sublime under this sky. It was raining. The scaffolding isn't fixed in the right place. I made a sketch which Darbon will send this evening to the workmen, who are living at Verberie.

Lady Diana Duff Cooper phoned this morning wanting me to dine at Chantilly. I phoned from the Grand Cerf to say it was impossible for me to leave work.

The hotel is full of the *Cyrano* cast, all complaining of the bad weather. Our chauffeur told me that Clément and Alekan weren't able to get the shot of the clouds this morning. The camera jammed, no doubt because of the vibration of the plane. They'll have to try again.

After dinner.

Interminable dinner. This hotel is alive with memories, for we camped here when we did *Baron Fantôme!* Every morning a bus used to take us through the rain into the courtyard of a Viollet-le-Duc château,[23] full of women extras wearing elaborate dresses and sitting about on the edge of wells. There we waited for the sun. Freezing draughts, enough to kill, swept through the vaults. We're to be awakened at six o'clock tomorrow. Jeannot's make-up takes three hours (apart from his hands). This evening the sky is overcast and the clouds tragic. A cold moon. It is autumn. I can see that the work isn't going to be too comfortable.

Monday the 24th, 6 o'clock.

Terrible night. My face and right hand itch. Gums. Eye. It was raining. And the misery of these germs preventing me from getting on with my work.

Monday, 11 o'clock.

Back to Senlis. Equinox. Heartbreaking rain. We left at 7:30. Found Rogelys in an inn a few kilometers outside Raray. Found the others eight kilometers further on, huddled together in another thieves' kitchen (out of a novel by Simenon). Brought Clément, his wife and Alekan back to Senlis. Darbon has gone off again to get Marais and Josette, who stayed at the first inn. Then we will lunch with the rest of the unit.

M. de Labédoyère told us: "Hunters know that it rains at the equinox for forty-eight hours. But it's taken me ten years to understand it. I always persisted."

Back at the Hôtel du Grand Cerf. Shall seize the opportunity to settle the three big trick shots at the end of the film. Alekan and Clément are both terribly upset because of yesterday morning. The clouds were splendid. The pilot perfect. The plane's vibration

[23][The French architect Eugène Emmanuel Viollet-le-Duc (1814–1879) heavily restored many châteaux in the course of his activities.]

upset the camera; it jammed, they could do nothing.

But to make up for this, they found a place in the forest which is just right for the Merchant to ride through on his horse and Beauty on Magnificent. Darbon urges us to shoot these exteriors by surprise tactics. We will abandon the studio on the first fine day we get.

The weather seemed to be clearing up. Now it's raining twice as hard.

6 o'clock.

Went on location hoping to do the takes of Marcel André, who, since he's playing at the Théâtre de la Michodière, is only free on Monday evenings. It rained, stopped raining, and rained again. In between two downpours the sky was in violent motion and threw a gloomy light onto the terrace of statues of hunting dogs and deer. But this lighting could not be filmed without being strengthened by electricity. Now, Darbon had given the electricians the day off this morning and they won't be here until seven o'clock tomorrow morning. We made the best of this dead time by plotting angles. I must admit that this day lost is a day gained for the film, since our work will be based on a scrupulous preparation without the least improvisation. I went home mad with toothache, beard sore, fingers itching and eyes aching. I didn't notice any of these miseries when we were in the midst of our work.

11 o'clock.

The doctor came to give Jean Marais a blood test. It looks as if another carbuncle is coming up near his ear. Marais, in spite of his courage, is visibly shaken by this appalling bad luck. The doctor prescribed a remedy to soothe my hand. Unfortunately, the ointment which he told me to get for my face is unobtainable. I must go on enduring this absurd torture. It's raining, raining. Will it be raining when we wake up? Marcel André must go back. We must take his two shots at any cost.

Tuesday the 25th.

On the eve of his execution, Ravaillac[24] said: "Tomorrow will

---

[24] [The religious fanatic who assassinated the French king Henri IV in 1610. His execution was spectacular.]

be rough going." It certainly has been. Rain. We set out. We reached Raray in a chaos of electrical installation, the mystery of cables and amperages. It was very cold. We dressed the artists in the great hall of the château, in the middle of which a ping-pong table stands. Jacques Lebreton, the sound chief, and the children of the family were having a game. Then they fixed up a table there out of planks and we ate a terrible ratatouille. I shot Marcel André's scene on the top of the wall with the perspective of the stone hounds. Then Marcel André below, between the vase and the pilaster. After that, I recorded his cries and the echo thrown between the park gate and the front of the château. Marcel changed, took off his make-up, had lunch, and then Darbon drove him back to Paris.

After lunch, at which Jeannot, made up as a ferocious beast, ate only biscuits and butter, we rehearsed the wall-of-busts scene. Rain. We ran for it. Parasols. The Labédoyère family and friends came to see us and take snaps of us all. When Antoine de Labédoyère heard that we were on a diet, he invited Marais and me to lunch tomorrow and the next day.

It cleared. The clouds were moving very quickly. The sun came out, then went in again. If it didn't rain again, it was ideal weather (apart from the cold) to shoot this sequence.

We tackled it at last; there were great difficulties with the sound, for the scene was interrupted several times by a wagon, a cow, a dog and a crying child.

Marais, visibly distressed by his make-up, was rebelling against himself. The result was a quiet tension, which showed through his normal interpretation of the part.

At six o'clock the workmen from the generating plant threatened to leave. We persuaded them to stay till 6:30. We took three shots. Two more would complete the scene. It was already evening. The arcades no longer opened onto trees but onto a hole of darkness. We lit smoke flares. Clouds formed behind the arcade where Marais stood silhouetted. Our shots are strange. Alekan is worried that his lights were too weak. As for me, I'm delighted with our angles and the liberties we've taken with the rules of film-making. Perhaps I won't be so pleased when I see the run-through. I was in agony with my teeth, ear and shoulder. My fingers were throbbing. My cheeks burning. I was shivering. I went back to the hotel and drank hot tea.

Josette and Jeannot have just left my room. I spoke to them a long time and ran through tomorrow's scene with them.

Wednesday the 26th, 7 a.m.

Pain all night. No sleep. My face was being devoured by some unknown germ, and my gums eaten into by some other. I had the sensation of inevitable disaster. I thought of dashing off to the dentist and the doctor in Paulvé's car. He should be coming to lunch at Raray.

This morning I have decided to try and hold out until the end of the takes. Unfortunately, it is raining. And we've still got two shots of yesterday's scene to do, and all those of the stag scene. It will be hopeless if it goes on raining. More and more time is being lost and the electricians can't fix the lamps. Marais and Josette are already on the set. I'll join them at nine o'clock.

11 p.m.

My face has become a carapace of cracks, ravines and itches. I must forget this mask and live underneath it as energetically as possible. Rained this morning, but the barometer was up. We built the scaffolding for the lights while the artists were making up and changing. At eleven o'clock we did the two shots still lacking in yesterday's scene. The last shot was very difficult owing to the smoke machines. Marais didn't use a stand-in. He himself did the jump from the arcade with the help of a springboard. After the takes we noticed, too late, that he'd carried his hat in his right hand yesterday, while today he didn't have it.

Marais and I lunched at Madame de Labédoyère's. A strange meal. I sat on the right of this old lady, who was dressed in black, and Marais on her left, made up as the Beast. I dare say her little girls will always remember it. After lunch I returned to the wall of busts (Paulvé ate in our communal dining room).

The two opening takes of the next scene were tricky. I wanted to introduce the scene with a shot of the stone and wood statue of the stag and finish it on the real stag. But the stag on the wall is very high up, and the cornice is very narrow. Josette climbed up. She was giddy. She didn't dare complain. She showed how really

A Raray exterior. The
Merchant on the statue
terrace (p. 45).

Hammond Collection

A Raray exterior. Beauty and the Beast (Jean Marais) in the park.

Hammond Collection

brave she is. We erected a scaffolding opposite for the cameraman and his assistants to roost beside their machine.

One of the advantages of making films is that you can mix, muddle up and reconstruct your place of action just as it suits you. This cresting of wall will become a ramp, this ramp will end in the balustrades which go round the château moat. Our last take of the evening was the walk seen through the balustrades. The only perfect take was spoiled by the laughter of some village child. The light, acting, movements, smoke machines, the tops of the trees crowned by sunlight, all collaborated for once. But in one second it was ruined. We can never hope to have such luck again. But no use crying about it, and no point in getting involved in that nightmare of running after it, persisting, or trying to recreate by an act of the will a group of harmonious circumstances which were only produced by chance. (It would only make the film seem labored.)

Thursday the 27th, 11 p.m.

The Labédoyère family have come to the conclusion that we are not a gang of hooligans. The film interests them and they're extremely hospitable. Josette, Jeannot, Darbon and I lunched with Antoine de Labédoyère this morning.

It threatened to be too fine. The clouds tore themselves apart to reveal a blue sky. Whereas, of course, the sequence we were doing needed a greyish half-light. But the weather improved—that is, got worse. We were back in the sombre light of the Beast's park.

Yesterday I jumped from the top of the wall to the edge of the balustrade. This morning I jumped from the edge of the balustrade to the arch of the terrace of statues that opens onto the trees. Heaven knows how I shall make it fit together. But I couldn't care less.

After the arch I passed on directly to the stairway, to the right of which the Beast is supposed to see the stag. The stag arrived in a little truck. There he was, lying down, tethered, with all his fabulous elegance and revolt.

I shot the close-up of Jeannot scenting the stag.

Clément, hidden behind the Beast's collar, animated his ears with a forked twig. They pricked up. The effect was striking.

The unit went to lunch. After lunch we shot the close-up of the

Beast's eyes. I was shown a rush of the close-up of the ears. I found it too diffuse and vague. We started it again, which put us behind schedule.

Escoffier confessed that the pearl necklace for Josette's silver dress was forgotten. My hands and face were causing me great pain, and I lost control. I got angry. Escoffier was in tears. I went on to the end of the scene where Josette pulls the Beast's sleeve, as he comes down from the pillar onto the steps; he takes his gloved fist from his face, she touches the glove with her fingers and together they come down the steps, as the camera trucks back at full speed. We lit the smokes and red powder. This made a shadow which we controlled by artificial light. The sky was pale blue, flecked with pink clouds, thin and in high relief. The red powder illuminated the leaves, the pompous smoke unfurled. I asked for action. But, alas, if it wasn't a guinea-fowl cackling, it was a tractor passing on the road, or a farmer bellowing at his cows. I persisted. Out of nine takes I got only two good ones. One trembles to think of the amount of sheer luck required before the director, the cameraman, artists and sound can all be satisfied.

Dull sky. Black trees. I wanted to take the shots of the stag. Two sturdy men had all their work cut out trying to hold him on the lawn in front of the château. In spite of his tether, he rolled over, wore himself out, writhed furiously. I gave it up. I'll take this shot in the Jardin des Plantes in Paris.

Which leaves for tomorrow morning the shot of Josette in her blue dress, running to look for the Beast; a back projection shot on the road and, if possible, another shot of Josette moving through the park. Whatever light we get tomorrow morning will determine entirely the style of the scene at the edge of the spring.

From this strange Raray, I shall bring back pictures which cannot be indifferent. Good or bad, but not mediocre. We've worked like demons.

Friday the 28th, 8 a.m.

My whole face is breaking out. It is covered with puffy areas, scabs and some flowing acid serum which tears up my nerves. I suppose I shall finish the exteriors this morning. Darbon has offered to take me back to Paris at eleven. What shall I do there? Just suffer in my room. R. can't see me until 7:30. The dentist

not till six o'clock. Better hang on till we finish here and go back
with the others. Jeannot's boil looks angry. He was as pale as death
when they took his mask off yesterday. The glue stops his circula-
tion. It's all a cruel struggle for the film. I wonder if I'll have to put a
stop to it. I'll take Jeannot to R. at 7:30. I have phoned Paul.

Before I finish with the statue terrace at Raray I must stop and
thank my unit from the bottom of my heart. They're serious, active,
easygoing, friendly. The least workman is gracious. Not one of
them has sulked in spite of this tedious shifting around of wires,
cameras and gear from one place to another, following orders
which, seen from the outside, seem sheer caprice. I have been
greeted only with smiles. Clément understands my style so well
that he could direct the scenes for me. Alekan knows in advance
the kind of strangeness that I'm after. Darbon puts up with my
tantrums and retakes. Aldo, our still photographer, who always
arrives at the moment when the edifice is crumbling, when the
groups are dispersing, puts on an act of bad temper that amuses the
cast and allows him to gain time and extract the last drops from the
squeezed lemon.

The make-up men and the dressers know their jobs. Lucile and
Escoffier carry their tiny mistakes as if they were a cross. In short,
the unit is an extension of myself. The old dream of forming one
person out of many is fully realized.

I'd be mad if I forgot that bad luck has always run through my
life. A sheer struggle. All striving and effort for even the simplest
things. I'd better expect difficulties in every guise. I must remember
this, and overcome them somehow.

This time they're in the guise of germs. But I can recognize them.
They don't deceive me. I will put up with this pain until it becomes
unbearable, but if it does it will be too bad. One can't alter a date.

If Marais can't go on filming it will be hopeless. If he can and
I'm too ill, I shall make arrangements to direct from a distance,
through Clément, whom I'm sure I can trust.

4 o'clock.

I shot in the rain without lights, using torches, magnesium and
English smoke-flares. Raray is in the can. I've simply thrown
myself against appalling conditions, and tried, whatever the cost,
to capture that fortuitous beauty which I like so much.

The workmen were wandering about with geese, rabbits and vegetables. It was all palavers, exchanges, parcels, baskets and string. Josette, wearing her silver dress, held a parasol, like the Negus,[25] as she stepped through beds of nettles.

We said goodbye to the Labédoyères. Marais, Darbon and Madame Clément went off in the car. Now it's my turn to disappear and restore the statue terrace to its shadows and solitude. My face is cracking, swelling, itching. I'm writing these lines at the hotel. Now I strap my bag and go.

Saturday the 29th.

Have seen Dr. R. He isn't very happy about my face. He's more optimistic about Jean Marais. Terrible night. I was really at the end of my tether. Darbon, Bérard, Alekan and Clément came to fetch me this morning. We went to Saint-Maurice. The décor's certainly odd but not in the way that the builders think. "That," said Bérard, "looks like Montboron."[26] We made them set the trees and gates up. The Merchant's hall is being built on a neighboring stage. Bérard is afraid that it is too much in the style of an inn, and wants it very simply furnished. The décor helps to set the right feeling. I am trying to get accustomed to the arrangement of the rooms, to live them while remembering the exteriors we took at Rochecorbon. Little by little, this dream I had is taking on a form and becoming fixed without losing its dream-like quality. Things arrive from a thousand different places all at once. By some sort of mysterious magnetism they fall into their right positions. I went back to the Palais-Royal for lunch. It was harder to bear the pain there than at work. At three I shall go to Epinay, where we can't start shooting till Wednesday through lack of current. We go to Joinville on Monday morning. (Noon–eight o'clock.)

Sunday.

Spent the day with doctors and Clément. Went over tomorrow's work: two large general shots of the sets, one at night (the Merchant's arrival), the other in the morning (the Merchant leaving, and the Beast's face). Have scrapped the gates. Will use

---

[25] [A title of the ruler of Ethiopia.]
[26] [On the Riviera, near Villefranche (see note on page 60).]

branches which part, showing the Beast's glaring eyes through them. Dined with Bérard and discussed the way the costumes should be worn. He'd prefer it if the Beast didn't have those enormous sleeves, but I'll keep them because I want the Beast to look as big as possible. I'll take them off in the shots of the great hall. I'm writing this waiting for the car. It's half past eight. We will have from nine to midday to get ready and then shoot from noon to eight. My forehead and eyes are now affected. R. says that the lower part of my face should respond to his treatment, but that I should go to a skin specialist for the upper part. How can I find the time to see all these doctors? Marais's boil is going on well. R. hopes that it will subside in five days. But meanwhile he must go on working under his mask. Doctors are costing us a fortune.

Monday, October 1st, 11 p.m.

The lower part of my face wasn't so bad this morning, but the upper part was inflamed and itching. I was at Saint-Maurice at nine. A veritable world of trained ants were swarming over the décor, and putting it just so. Gradually ivy, brambles and grass invaded the sets, making them look like ruins. Moss and dead leaves covered the ground. The lights were hoisted up, flew away and hid everywhere. A huge awning extended the studios right to the alley wall. The camera was to truck back there. The studio door had been taken off its hinges to reveal an avenue of trees. Branches had been fixed up to open and close as if by magic. The château was wrapped in shadows, thanks to the smoke machines. The first take was of the angles of the stones with the moon on them. The Merchant comes in through a fog scattered by ventilators. The branches draw aside, he goes in. Then the branches close behind him.

Endless preparation. Alekan complaining that he hasn't enough arcs; Darbon sulking; Clément unwell—he's in for a bout of flu. Tiquet, who arrived this morning, rescued us with his fresh new ideas. Jean Marais was made up—it took four hours because of his hands and claws.

About six o'clock we shot Marcel André leaving on Magnificent, the branches closing again, Marais parting them and (close-up) watching him ride away. We intended to take this close-up of Marais in shadow, with only his eyes lit, by reflecting an arc-lamp

onto them. But there wasn't time. We'll have to keep this effect
for some other occasion.

At 1:30 we saw the first rushes of the stuff we shot at Raray.
I think they are very beautiful, and Marais's voice struck me as
most impressive. It's the voice of an invalid, of a monster in pain.
We will see the rest tomorrow evening. We left at nine. We dined
at the Palais-Royal. I went to bed.

Tuesday evening, Oct. 2nd, 10 o'clock.

Got to the studio at midday. They're fixing the camera rails
up for the Merchant shot. I had lunch, after which I did the shot of
the stable and the shot of the frightened Merchant going up the
steps. That finishes with Marcel André. Now for the really difficult
stuff: Josette and Jeannot. Moonlight. I was determined to do my
six shots in spite of Alekan being so slow, and the arcs, which kept
on fusing. When we got to the shot where the Beast carries Beauty,
Jeannot, tangled in his own sleeves and Josette's cape, couldn't lift
her up and walk. Out of superstition, I hid so the take would be
successful. It was. I set up the camera at the top of the stairs and did
the shot of the Beast carrying Beauty, who is tattooed by the
shadows of the leaves in the moonlight.

At 7:30, run-through of the Raray stuff. It depressed me beyond
words. Some negatives had been scratched in the lab. I was
trembling before every shot. Luckily the negatives I liked best
aren't scratched, but you can see faint marks on them. There must
have been a mechanical accident in the lab, but they won't admit
it, and say it's due to bad stock. The proof is that the rushes we saw
the day before yesterday were neither scratched nor marked.

The general effect is "beautiful," too flat and grey. The château
looks like a sketch for a stage-set. I had begged Alekan not to over-
light, but just pick out certain angles in relief. But cameramen are
always afraid of the new but often admirable idea. I didn't leave the
projection room in complete despair, for I can still make a
sensational montage out of it.

Wednesday, 8 a.m.

I am tackling Epinay this morning. (The gate. The Merchant's
first sight of the Beast. The scene with the rose.) The weather looks

brilliant. The sun will help us. I will take only the shots of Marcel André. Jeannot's resting. His boil's enormous. It looks as if he won't be able to go on playing Avenant—in which case it will be the insurance company that's called.

Wednesday evening, 6 o'clock.

Bérard and I reached Epinay at nine. We found the studio exactly as it was a fortnight ago. The workmen had an enormous role to play here. In two hours these trained ants painted the gate, built the pyramids, thinned the grass, suppressed some trees and created others, constructed overhead scaffolds and loaded them with lights. At four o'clock they were still at it, and the carcass hadn't arrived. There's a strike at Les Halles. At six o'clock I told everybody they could go and pointed out that the firm was to blame for this wasted day. We will begin again tomorrow morning.

Paulvé, who had come to have lunch with us, said, "What! haven't you done any shots this morning?" I wonder what he'll have to say this evening.

A projection with Ibéria and Clément at 6:15. I realized what a complete disaster the Raray stuff is. I'll have to make do with what I can't do without, and by prodigious cutting I'll scrap the worst of it. Fortunately, the things I liked best have turned out all right. I was pleased with yesterday's rushes, but after the Raray fiasco I no longer dare entertain the least hope. I have found the beginning of the rose scene. As the Merchant steps forward, the rose lights up. He looks at it. And the rose illuminates everything: the gate, the trees, etc. . . . This means I shall be able to cut from the grey scene to the bright scene without any hitch.

Thursday morning, 8 o'clock.

Paulvé gave lunch yesterday at the bistrot in Epinay for important members of his board of directors and the press. Mounier said to me: "We're counting on your work to re-establish French films." To which I replied: "It's funny that I, who am attacked on every side in France should, at the same time, be looked to to save the prestige of a country which calls me names. I shall do my best to make a film that will please me and the people I like. More than that, I don't promise."

Film people are charming. Everybody, down to the least work-man, calls me "General"—it's an old gag of theirs. They speak to me with *tu* and *toi*, but that familiarity doesn't mean they don't carry out my orders at once. An outsider might say that the studio looked chaotic but this chaos soon disappears. All the gear gets fixed, trees, flower-beds, sets, and even the invisible strings to open the door, gravitate to their right positions.

Yesterday, for the first time, an all-essential prop wasn't to hand: the dead deer. The manager for exteriors, who was responsible for obtaining this, didn't even dare show his face again. I waited in the street outside the studio. His only excuse was the strike at the market. But in the film world one asks for something and gets it, no matter what. We shall see if I get my dead deer this morning.

A film is a monument, but built neither in the present, past or future.

Thursday evening, 11 o'clock.

My head is spinning after a killing day. A hunt through Les Halles for a dead deer. Couldn't be found. Then to Epinay. Where the current went off. We waited. Drizzle. Then eventually Darbon turned up, bringing me some dead dogs, which stank so horribly I couldn't use them. I asked Clément to bring them back to the slaughterer and have them skinned. The current was still off. Lunch. The current came on again. The rose scene was ready. Clément came back sick after what he'd seen at the slaughterer's. After lunch I was told that I had a dead deer. I went back to the gate scene. Alekan set up the lights. The current went off again. I phoned the power station. The failure would continue all day. Dead day. We dragged around and left at five. The projection room at Paulvé's was available. I dashed into it to see the day-before-yesterday's rushes. A poor projection but I could see the mistakes I had made. Marais was right. I ought to do a close-up of Josette looking frightened, to come after the shot where he says: "Where are you going?" The negative was bad. I couldn't see any trace of the powerful arcs we used. The staircase which Josette comes down was too much to the left of the picture. I went off to R. in despair of ever finding perfection that can overcome its difficulties. It's always just beyond one's reach. Sometimes one can almost touch it. But something is lacking. Perhaps with this soft stock we'd better triple the lights and print dark. If I go on struggling I shall end up by finding my dream again but at the cost of what exhaustion! I am going to bed with my forehead burning with the rash, completely done in.

Friday, Oct. 5th, 8 a.m.

Hardly slept a wink. The film went round and round in my mind, facing me with all its faults. Alekan hasn't enough confidence. He keeps hesitating and won't take a bold enough line. The result is a certain softness in his work which I must try to correct. It's all too "beautiful." I would like it harsher, with more contrast. I'll keep at him till he gets it.

Friday, 9 p.m.

My struggle with destiny continues. Not a cloud in the sky this morning when I reached Epinay. Preparations for work went quickly. The ventilator was set up. I shot the rose scene. Four shots, including the one of the dead deer. I opened its throat myself and poured the hemoglobin on it. Some beautiful patches of sunlight through the leaves. Stopped for lunch at midday. Had just started again at 1:30 (at which rate I should have got my nine shots in the can) when the current went off again. Couldn't get any clear statement over the phone, except that the breakdown would probably last till six o'clock. I drove the unit over to Saint-Maurice. I wanted to see the last batch of rushes again, stop them from demolishing the whole of the old set, and supervise the new set. I told Alekan off after the run-through. His mania for plotting his shots, yet at the same time making them appear diffuse, revolts me. It's all too "artistic". Nothing is equal to the sublimation of the documentary style. It is this style I want from him.

Patience is essential to this profession. You must wait. Always wait. Wait for the car that's coming to fetch you. Wait till the lights are fixed. Wait till the camera's ready. Wait while branches are nailed to their supports. Wait for sunlight. Wait for the scene painters. Wait. Wait till it's developed. Wait for the sound track to be married to the picture. Wait till the projection room's free. Wait while the projectionist changes the lamps which have just fused. Wait. Wait. Wait.

This way our patience is proved, and our nerves tried. Nerves twisting this way, then that way. I shall start out tomorrow morning at 8:30, not knowing whether the current will be on or not. The city people never warn us but just cut it off when it suits them and ruins our work. They don't give a damn. We used to say: "It's the Germans." Today we wonder through what malice, what sabotage, French activities are being disorganized.

Big photograph of Jeannot as the Beast on the first page of *Samedi Soir*. The other photographs are undistinguished and the article "picturesque" and inaccurate. My article and a page by Bérard in *Images de France*. We are getting phone calls from all over the place for articles and photos. The film is exciting considerable curiosity.

Saturday the 6th, 9 p.m.

Thanks to my idea of sending for Josette we've made up our schedule. Marcel André was filming the reverse shots for the scene where the Beast first shows himself and causes a terrible gust of wind to arise. This terrible wind came from a wind machine, in front of which I threw handfuls of dead leaves. The wind snatches Marcel's hat off as though the Beast were obliging him to stand at the ready. Marcel was through at one o'clock. After lunch I shot the end of the rainy scene at Raray. Beauty, walking alone in the park, surprises the Beast drinking. I intended to light this scene with magnesium flares but couldn't find any more, and the red powder burns too quickly. So I used arcs and just a few lamps. Smoke drifted. Josette goes toward the gate. She hears a lapping noise. She approaches the gate. I cut. Close-up. She half-opens the gate. An arc strikes her face. She looks. She shuts the door and turns away. I cut. Facing the path, I shot her walking in a daydream until her face blocked the camera lens. Michel de Brunhof came to watch us film and to choose some of Aldo's stills for *Vogue*.

There's going to be no current on Monday. We'll film tomorrow, Sunday.

Sunday the 7th, 8 a.m.

The car came for Marais at 6:45. His make-up (I will show his hands today) will take four hours. I am writing these few lines waiting for the car that's due here at the Palais-Royal at 8:30. I have just written the preface for poor Georgette Leblanc's book, *La Machine à Courage*. Yes, certainly this woman[27] was a dynamo of courage. I must imitate her.

In spite of being ravaged with rashes and all sorts of pains, I persist. I continue. And this desperation suits me. It certainly is no effort for me. My work is that of an archeologist. The film exists (pre-exists). I have to unearth it from the shadow where it sleeps, with a pick and shovel. Sometimes I spoil it by being too hasty. But the fragments left intact shine with the beauty of marble.

When you think of the number of fortuitous circumstances that have to happen simultaneously, at the same second, if a shot is to be a success, you can hardly imagine it'll ever occur. But when it does, even this prodigious good luck is subject to further dangers. The indifference of machines. If the electricity is cut when the negative is in the bath, the work is ruined. You are never safe. Retakes cost a fortune. The sets are demolished. The spirit is burnt out. I'm well aware that great things are expected from this film. I must arm myself against the fear this expectation causes me. It would make me timid. I must work as I did at the time of *Le Sang d'un Poète*, when no one was watching me. That is the way to achieve freshness.

Waiting for the car yesterday, I wrote the article which Brunhof wanted for *Vogue* on the wife of the English ambassador. She wanted the article to be by me. She's another dynamo of courage. Her large blue eyes—a blue as vivid as scarlet—defy ridicule. She maintains the style of ambassadors' wives who prefer tradition to modernity.

We are all paying now for five terrible years. "To make bad blood" isn't a mere figure of speech. For that is precisely what we all made, and it's this bad blood which now disintegrates us. Five years of hate, fear, a waking nightmare. Five years of shame and slime. We were spattered and smeared with it even to our very souls. We had to survive. Wait. It is this nervous waiting that we are paying for dearly. In spite of all difficulties, we must catch up. Whatever the cost, France must shine again. I dare say America can't begin to understand what we have to overcome, what it's

[27][Celebrated Belgian-born French actress and singer (1869–1941), who was married to the playwright Maurice Maeterlinck from 1901 to 1918. The book of her memoirs with Cocteau's preface appeared in 1947.]

like trying to work a ramshackle machine without oil. Our work-men's skill saves us. It's beyond praise.

My beard's white. I didn't suspect that. Well, there it is, my beard's white. That isn't serious. It would be a serious matter if my soul was just as faded. Thank God my blood's still red. I'll pour it out to the last drop. I'll not spare any.

Sunday, 7:30 p.m.

At last we have just left that terrible studio at Epinay, a sort of sewer surrounded by trains, buses, woodcutters and guinea-fowl. Only comparison sound can be recorded there. I had to let Marcel André go at one o'clock as he's playing in *Vient de Paraître*.[28] At twelve the current went off and I still had to do one of the shots showing the storm and his terror when he first sees the Beast. By a miracle the current came on again so we just made it. Lunch. Marais, made up, his hands done, furious because his nails won't stick on, refused to come with us and shut himself up in his dressing room. They took him some purée and stewed fruit without sugar, as this ferocious beast is on a diet, and anyhow he can't open his mouth without disturbing his make-up.

At two o'clock we started the shots of Marais alone. The apprentice dressed as the Merchant will appear at the edge of the frame. I found some very striking angles, but daren't hope for too much, remembering what surprises the Kodak film stock and the lab can produce. I can only wait and see. Once Marais had his long hair on, his temper seemed to be shorter, and he bristled at the slightest word. He was upset by this too. He took himself in hand and then started behaving that way again. It was exhausting racing to finish by 6 p.m. To all this, Alekan remained as indifferent as any cameraman. Sound ready to go again. Then an arc fused. Marais forgot his lines. Darbon's face fell. I got worked up. Arakelian started retouching Marais's make-up just as I was about to shoot. If I had reprimanded him, Marais would have been angry. In short, we proceeded from one crisis to another till we filmed the last shot, where the Beast's right hand comes toward the camera in close-up.

I gave the workmen a drink all round and then left this detestable studio for ever. Tomorrow, Monday, nothing's doing. We'll start

[28][A stage comedy by Edouard Bourdet (1887–1945), originally produced in 1927.]

The set with the door of the Beast's castle. The Merchant approaches
cautiously (p. 52).

The forest set (p. 64),
with the Merchant who
has lost his way.

Hammond Collection

again on Tuesday morning and do the father's room (tear scene) at Saint-Maurice, which is a studio I like. Yesterday La Victorine Studios at Nice were burned down.

Monday the 8th, 10 a.m.

I shall spend the day resting, seeing doctors. I will go to the dentist, R., Clément Simon. My eyes were sore last night and I couldn't read yesterday. I had to get Clément to read the report of Laval's trial to me in the car. This is a case brought by politics against *policy*. Laval swims very well in dirty water. Others go under in it.

Yesterday was a fête for the dogs, Moulouk and Ficelle (Lucile's dog). They were delighted with the carcasses of the deer and the dogs. They simply rolled in them.

To be honest, I just wouldn't know what to do without this film work. I can't wake from this dream and jump back with both feet into life. Besides, I'm hardly presentable except to those who are used to my miseries. I look very strange, what with my forehead, eyes and white beard. The world is such that it would simply think I was trying to look eccentric. So I keep myself to myself.

I skipped my appointment with the dentist after all and went to Joinville with Bérard. I wanted to go over the Merchant's house thoroughly, furnish it, soak myself in its atmosphere: *live* it. Bérard arranged the furniture. I had to see R. at 5:30. I left Bérard in the middle of doing the father's room, where I'll be shooting tomorrow. Just got back from seeing R. and Clément Simon. The latter loathes R. He thinks the sulphanilamides have caused this skin disease. An unfair diagnosis, since I had the dermatitis before I started to use this Septoplix. I have to treat this dermatitis with cold compresses which are hard on the infectious spots. Simple as this treatment is, it's almost impossible when filming because one can't rest, diet or keep anything sterile.

A studio is the very antithesis of a clinic. Only people with iron constitutions can stick it, invalids certainly can't. In fact, they're not welcome.

Tuesday the 9th, 11 p.m.

A good day full of the kind of work I like. Everything went as well as could be expected. The studio was cold owing to the wet plaster. It warmed up once the lights were on. The room, soon reduced to chaos by having to move things around to get at the right shooting angle, looked like a Vermeer sacked by vandals. Marcel André slept right through all this with the sheets right up to his chin. We kept the floor tiles covered with paper except when they had to be shown. Bérard arrived in the truck at nine. Josette was there at seven; I, at 8:30. It always takes such a time to get a set ready. By midday, we'd only done the shot which comes before the special effect (yet to be done) when Josette passes through the wall. The camera pans round the room, comes to rest for a second on the sick father sleeping, then moves at top speed toward the wall. Will start the trick shot with this same swift camera movement so as to link up. After lunch I did the shot of Josette kneeling beside the bed. It was getting on for six and the union won't let us go a second over time. At seven minutes to six Alekan was still setting the lights on Josette for the shot that follows the trick. She must sparkle. At two minutes to six she sparkled, and I put in the can the shot of her coming forward, taking her glove off, throwing it on the bed and kneeling down.

In order to get enough room for the trucking rails we had to break through partitions and move furniture around. This set, which was so carefully put together, became a shambles. We reflected patches of light from large water vats and bits of broken mirror over the characters so as to give them the appearance of luminous marble as in the ceilings at Villefranche.[29] Gradually I am coaxing my myths and childhood memories back again. If only I have managed to fix them onto the screen. I'm not sure I have.

Wednesday the 10th, 8:30 a.m.

I must not complain. I must pay. I must accept the risks. The irritation on my face is unbearable. My eyes, ears and arms are also affected. The only thing to do is to work so hard I forget it. I made a mistake yesterday. I shot the father's bedroom with the furniture which had been taken away by the money-lender. Therefore I must transform my mistake into a discovery. When Beauty comes

[29][Villefranche-sur-Mer, on the Riviera between Nice and Monte Carlo, where Cocteau went during his first opium addiction cure in 1925. It was while staying at the Hôtel Welcome there that he met Bérard. He spent much time there on and off in the following years, and wrote several of his most important works there.]

back, so must the furniture return too, by magic. This afternoon, we must show the room suddenly emptying again before Ludovic confesses that he's signed the bond.

Wednesday evening, 11 o'clock.

I've been worried all day by an oppressive sense, which is neither a critical sense nor common sense. I was out of touch with the work. The set-builders stood around in groups because of union meetings. The film seemed moribund. The lugubrious grey light I detest enveloped the artists even when Alekan raked them with arcs. The arcs sizzled and spoiled the good takes. Josette couldn't go on kneeling. A fake diamond has no fire to it; only a real diamond sparkles. I'm afraid I'll have to correct the takes of the diamond. I couldn't do the last scene. Time was up. The lamps went off. I went over my directions for tomorrow morning's scene— Ludovic with the bailiffs.

Run-through. Some of it's superb. Some of it is grey and dim. Is this the lab's fault? I hope so. I'll ask them to print with more contrast. I'll try to obtain artificially the contrasts Kodak stock is incapable of getting.

My beard is growing. My forehead is peeling. My boils are multiplying. I struggle on. I have been given the book about myself written by Lannes and published by Seghers.[30]

Thursday morning the 11th, 7 o'clock.

I woke up this morning after a night in which my dreams were shaken like dirty water forming absurd patterns. My neck hurts. The boil which started yesterday on the back of my neck is bigger. The pain is trying to find my weakest point in its effort to overcome me. I'll fight the germs as long as I can, but they are stronger than we are. We will work from nine to 4:30. The studio hands are knocking off for a union meeting. On Saturday the sound people, who are stupidly paid, are going on strike. I'll shoot the silent linking-up shots of the stag and Josette's faint. It's all a struggle, internal and external. Everything conspires against this film.

[30][*Jean Cocteau*, by Roger Lannes, in the series *Poètes d'aujourd'hui*, 1945.]

Thursday evening.

This morning I shot the scene which was left over yesterday evening (the one where the bailiffs carry off the chest and Ludovic comes in and confesses to his father). After lunch we all went on to the great hall set. Bérard arrived and thought the dresses were in a bad state; he divided his time between them and the set. The slightest breach of taste would turn it into "Ye Olde Inn." No need to worry with this simple furniture and the Vermeer-like arrangement of the objects which Bérard evoked in a few minutes. Then we went to deal with the extravagant forest set which I'm having built on a neighboring stage for the horseback sequence where the Merchant loses his way in the mist. I do admire the workmen; they achieve the impossible. They recreate a nature that fools the animals. Dogs scratch at the foot of the fake trees. The horse nibbles the fake branches.

I climbed ladders and reached the top of a veritable mountain of wood and plaster. With Clément and Alekan I found some angles which I could never have visualized from the ground. Sound goes on strike Saturday. I shall take the opportunity to do silent takes of the Merchant wandering in the wood and getting lost.

The choice of what we can do is narrowed down, what with Marais's illness and the (less serious) state of the dresses. It's out of the question to make Jeannot work. Impossible to use some of the dresses. I'll shoot something or other.

I can't praise Josette enough. Except for one or two, where she looks too big, all the scenes I ran through of her yesterday evening are adorable. Her acting is grace, simplicity, the natural-supernatural itself. She is a good little girl talking to her father and telling him things he cannot understand, yet she doesn't overwhelm him with her splendor. I'm enormously indebted to Pagnol.[31] The tear effect has come off better than we'd dared hope.

Friday, Oct. 12th, 11 p.m.

A major problem is finding one's way about in this mix-up of time and remembering which dress and what hair style the actresses must wear to correspond with the scene that goes before and the

---

[31][Marcel Pagnol, the famed author, director and producer (born 1896).]

one that will come after. This morning I could indulge in the luxury of transforming Mila. We had brought Bérard out to Saint-Maurice. He shut himself up in her dressing room with her. An hour later an absolute marvel appeared, a Spanish portrait of extreme nobility and as violent as a caricature. The actress's little doll-like head was framed by the cone of a high wig, studded with red ribbons and diamonds, and a ruff starched, shaped, boned, waved, curled and furled like a submarine plant.

This was for the five-o'clock dinner scene, with Beauty serving at table and then running off when her sisters insult her. Which links up to her scene with Jeannot which we took at Rochecorbon — and which is so bad I intend to do it over again.

I urged Alekan to get plenty of contrast into this scene.

At five o'clock the men started putting up enough scaffolding to besiege a whole town, and in less time than it took the actors to make up. This scaffolding blocked the stairs, forced us to get together by means of ladders, and allowed us to push the trucking rail up to the two inmost corners of the first floor. There I placed the scene of the sisters leaving Beauty's room and the scene where they meet Ludovic, who asks them for the golden key. I had hoped to do one more scene: the one where Ludovic runs upstairs after his sister, who won't listen to him. It required a new construction in perspective. It was six and we had to stop at half past, so it was too late. I stopped and went wandering in my forest. I will shoot Marcel André on the horse there tomorrow. My beard's growing longer. My cheeks thinner. But the film has to decrease and fill out.

Saturday, Oct. 13th, 8 a.m.

We're going to work on the forest today from midday till 8 p.m. Alekan is to be at Saint-Maurice by nine to set up his arcs on scaffolds and do his tetrachloride tests. (Like the boom and the wind machine, the fog gadget's out of order.) I'm resting and taking this opportunity to review the situation. I haven't the remotest idea how the film as a whole will turn out. Each shot has been caught on the wing with all the intensity and passion that I can summon. I have made my selection from the stuff I shot in Touraine but not yet from Raray, Epinay or Saint-Maurice. I'd like to do this in the course of a long session, permeated by the style of the film, so I won't be tempted by a shot merely because it's good photography. It's possible that slowness will result from all this speed, from all these short scenes. Nobody can foretell. It's a question I refuse to worry about. I work from day to day and try to aim at a single target at every given moment. It would be strange if some beauty doesn't emerge from such a collection of takes. Ibéria assures me that it will. But in this profession people can be mistaken even when they imagine things are certain. Sometimes I catch myself saying: "As far as I'm concerned, that shot was perfect" after a bad take. Sometimes I have bad takes printed and find that they're good.

Sunday, Oct. 14th, 6 p.m.

I was too ill to write yesterday evening. For the first time, pain triumphed all along the line. At night, with the magnification that comes in the night, I thought that the boil on the back of my neck was becoming some sort of phlegmon, and that I'd have to stop working. It's true that, thanks to my unit, even if I did, the work could go on. Marais could coach the actors, Clément could handle the general direction, Ibéria the continuity. Bérard would contribute the miraculous. My unit is good enough to go on for a week without me and, as Madame de LaFayette[32] says: *"par machine."*

A blood test this morning. R. at five. I'm very, very ill. At seven, Dr. Chabannier told me the result of the analysis: sugar's there again and encourages the germs to make this offensive. I shall have to start the insulin again.

I shall go to the studio as long as I am able. But go I will.

Tackled the forest set yesterday. It's a complete artificial world of grass, moss, rocks and bark. The groom who brought Marcel's horse took one look at the set, then disappeared on the sly, frightened that we wanted to make his horse do acrobatics. When I arrived: no horse. We looked for the horse. Cars dashed off in every direction. At last it was found. We soothed the groom. Things were arranged, but so late that the six shots we planned were reduced to two. I will shoot the rest, and Josette, with stand-ins. The fog and the distance will enable me to get away with it. After that extension piece, I will do the sisters' room.

Nothing's more mysterious than the photograph. I'm looking

32[Celebrated author of *La Princesse de Clèves* (1634–1693).]

at my photo on the cover of *Le Monde Illustré*. I was in Touraine. I thought I was cured. I was about to become quite ill. The camera could see what I couldn't. I thought I was perfectly fit but it's a photo of a sick man.

Unless the situation changes, I was right to fight against diffuse lighting and the use of gauzes. Yesterday's pictures were a thousand times more robust and showed that clean, sculptured line in the bright areas which I admired so much in Périnal.[33] It isn't kind to the women but it does bring out their character. Alekan is gradually finding his balance and a style that corresponds to the way I tell a story, gesticulate or write. He's most attentive and I'm very grateful to him. He's never stubborn and doesn't try to prove I'm wrong. Our unit is becoming more and more homogeneous.

Monday, October 15, 1945.

A day in the forest, which was rather damp. A plaster forest where the cold strikes up through your shoes, which isn't exactly good for a cold. I was always without either one horse or the other. Groups of unknown sightseers drifted through my trees, climbed over my hillocks and got in the workmen's way. They were armed with Kodaks. I worked as best I could in the fog and the flashing arcs. I'll use what I consider successful in a quick montage. Marais's still got his boil. Mila is ill, with a temperature of 102. I think we'll have to call in the insurance company again. I finished off with a bird's-eye pan shot of Josette's stand-in on Aramis taken from one of the little trucks slung between two high scaffolds. If Mila's illness keeps me from making a start on the sisters' room tomorrow, I'll go on with the forest. I'll try to do some close-ups which will come in handy when editing. I had an appointment at Joinville with Ibéria at 10:30 to choose the Raray, Epinay and Saint-Maurice takes. First class run-through. Alekan has got what I wanted. — My boils exhaust me. I start on insulin again tomorrow.

Tuesday, October 16, 1945.

I'm not in the least proud of the fact, but I wonder who else would work as I work, suffering as I suffer? What I mean is, I

---

[33] [Georges Périnal (born 1897), the great cinematographer who had done the photography of *Le Sang d'un Poète*.]

wonder if there is any professional in this field in which I work only rarely who'd exert himself at the cost of all his strength, preferring the work to his own health. Living in this chaos of set-builders, electricians, wardrobe mistresses, make-up men, decorators, assistant decorators, in this cyclone of dust and moving furniture, the back of my neck devoured by a vicious beast and riddled by a star of pain which flashes its fires into the nerves of my skull and shoulders. And a cold besides, an incurable cold, which, though it always raises a laugh in the theater, like cuckolds and deaf people, isn't so funny for all that. I wonder what would happen to me if it weren't for Jean Marais's devotion and kindness? He looks after me though he's ill himself, and comes to Saint-Maurice to give me my insulin injections.

Did the sisters' room today. In one hour, while I was choosing the takes with Ibéria in the projection room, Bérard gave it the elegance, comfort and peculiar disorder which any room has that's well lived in.

"If you get through your seven scenes," Paulvé promised, "I will leave your forest intact." I made it by combining three shots in one. The camera sees Cabriole, the arrow landing in the room and the table being overturned, then pans up to Nane Germon crying "My dress!" The third time around Jacinthe refused to stay on the cushion. She knew what was coming.

Projection: the forest in the fog. Some of it's all right, but I haven't got enough for editing. The producers will have to realize that it's sheer madness to spend a fortune on building a set and then do a rush job.

Wednesday, October 17, 1945, 11 p.m.

In the sisters' room I was able to follow the work stretched out on one of the beds with yellow canopies. Of course, the back of my neck kept me from stretching out. I did some fairly simple scenes which are to form a contrast to more unusual scenes. By 6:15 I had accomplished my schedule, which means I can take my time tomorrow and go easier.

Saw Dr. D. (specialist on boils) at eight o'clock. The diet we'd been following amazed him. He told us to drop it and started giving me injections to clean my blood up and act as a tonic.

Thursday, 4 a.m.

Woke up with unbearable pain. As I can neither sleep nor walk up and down, I calm myself by picking up this notebook and trying to shout my pain to the unknown friends who will read these lines. They exist. I know them without knowing them. I make them out in the darkness. A ferocious beast (the Beast) has got its paw on the nape of my neck and is torturing me. The carbuncle is just getting a root and legions of enemy germs encircle it, to protect me. A furious battle which for me takes place in one night, for the germs over years, generations, which build a positive Wall of China around the pain. I have just taken some pyrethane. In spite of my courageous resolutions, despite my certainty that I am paying for the too great pleasure of directing a film which I'd dreamt about for months and months, it is difficult for me to live these minutes. The pain forces me to complain. A cruel thorn, deep roots, a coral of fire, on top of the burning bush of my sick nerves. My ears are throbbing. How can I go on bearing this? What can I do? I must go on. And now the light's gone off. — I thought it might stay off all night, but now it's back. I will try to draw my torture.

There are plumes of pain, smoke-clouds of pain, flourishes, lightnings and illuminations of pain. Last night about nine, Huisman and Cohen came to see me about their project of a documentary film on my work. They saw the state I was in when I came back from the doctor. And after staying about five minutes they went off again.

I never thought I would have to comfort myself again by doing these drawings, as I used to in the days when I was under Doctors Dereck and Solier.[34] Then I was being cured of opium addiction. Perhaps these carbuncles are a similar cure, as my system casts out the toxins of its nutriments and disgust with life.

Thursday evening, 11 o'clock.

Dr. Dumas can't give me the sulphate of copper injections because the nettle-rash has started again on my eyes. The lesion on the nape of my neck is still very hard and painful. Our work today was difficult since the electricity broke down every other hour.

---

[34][Cocteau underwent opium addiction cures in 1925 and 1928. He published the drawings he made during the 1928 cure (at Saint-Cloud, outside Paris) in the book *Opium* (1930).]

All the same I managed to get into the can the scene where Nane ties the velvet bows on Mila's pointed wig. I had placed basket-work and wires in front of the arcs, to throw shadows like that of the cages onto the actresses' faces.

After lunch, I tackled the hall scene where the sisters come back from the stable with the magic mirror. Finished up at six by doing the monkey which Mila sees in the mirror when she looks into it. He was a charming creature. I did this shot by putting an ordinary glass into the mirror frame and placing the monkey behind it. We made him wear a bonnet like the sisters', put a ruff round his neck and sat him on an open book à la Chardin.[35]

Tomorrow morning I'll do the old hag whom Nane sees. After that I'll deal with the sequence of the Merchant coming home after seeing the Beast. (The scenes where Marais is shown only in profile or three-quarters.)

Friday evening, midnight.

If I wrote every evening: "I have finished my seven shots. I have finished such and such a scene," it would be tedious. The essential thing is to try and make young people, who will one day read me, realize that heroism is the natural condition of the poet, that the poet is only a servant of the power of a force that drives him and that a true servant never abandons his master, but follows him even to the scaffold. My pain was so violent during work today that I was afraid, all the time, that I was going to faint. But I continued, directed, invented and received visitors as if I had an inexhaustible supply of energy. Several times I seemed to be feeling the effects of an anesthetic: the commotion of our work suddenly appeared to have an incredible vulgarity and *sameness*. We were rushing headlong into a world of multiplicity, delicacy and secrecy beside which all our clutter looked like a farce in bad taste. I suppose it was a faint coming on. But our world exists, we must be modest about it. I didn't stop telling them where to place the camera, directing the cast, running to fetch them from their dressing rooms, seeing the rushes and trying to hurry Alekan and Aldo, who are both slowness itself. I have set myself against that tribunal which condemns anything out of the ordinary to torture. I'm determined to accomplish the exceptional. It is the

[35] [The Louvre possesses a painting by Jean Chardin (1699–1779) showing a monkey as a painter.]

one privilege still left to France.

Saturday morning, the 20th.

Last night was so unbearable that I was almost happy. It was the hair shirt, the ecstasy of a monk. In *Le Sang d'un Poète* the statue says: "You have written that you walked through a mirror but you didn't believe it." It would be ridiculous to write "a poet must be a saint" and then complain just when circumstances force us to prove it. I look at myself in the mirror. It's awful. But it doesn't worry me in the slightest. The physical doesn't matter any more. Artistic creation and its beauty must take its place. It would be criminal to make the film suffer from my suffering and ugliness. The movie screen is the true mirror reflecting the flesh and blood of my dreams. As for the rest, that doesn't matter any more.

On top of everything, I have tracheitis. I keep coughing and each cough makes the open wounds hurt more. If I were in good health perhaps the film would be ill. I am paying. Paying in cash. Which is the moral of *Les Chevaliers de la Table Ronde*,[36] a play that nobody understood, because at that time nobody would take anything seriously or make the slightest effort. — A work which devours its author isn't a joke. It is a truth. The work of art hates us and contrives by any foul means to get rid of us.

Sunday the 21st.

Yesterday things reached a crisis. It was as though my neck were being sawn through with a blunt saw. After lunch, I was drunk, sick, with pain. I thought I was going to faint. I could see from the way the workmen looked at me that they were afraid of it too. Their kindness is unending. Raymond Méresse, the chief electrician, brought some fresh lard, which one can't get anywhere. I have to put it on my face every night. All the same, I was able to pull myself together enough to direct the scene preceding Marais's slapping Mila's face and to find good positions for the camera.

An endless stream of visitors from Switzerland and Belgium (*Formes et Couleurs*,[37] etc. . . .), all interested in the film and wanting

[36] [Play by Cocteau, 1937, in which Jean Marais made his début (as Galahad).]
[37] [Magazine published in Lausanne.]

photographs. One thing that delighted me at the run-through is that we don't have the desire of creating tableaux, or "paintings." They arise naturally from the scenes and do not dominate them. The danger with cinema work is that if you try to achieve a Rembrandt you end up with a Roybet.[38] It's better not to think about it, then sometimes you obtain Vermeers.

Yesterday I had my beard shaved, which immediately relieved me of a terrible itch, as each hair was an antenna of pain. In 1945 it costs 200 francs to have a shave.

This morning Nane Germon took us to a restaurant that makes a specialty of oysters, as my new doctor has recommended them. I don't like appearing in public. The Parisian public is tactless, cruel and amused by pain. In the Métro yesterday evening a young captain, realizing that I couldn't stand, offered me his seat. I couldn't get over it. Generally my bandages only make people laugh.

Sunday evening.

My eye is affected now and is swollen up as if it had been whipped with nettles.

Monday the 22nd, evening.

The pain is now a torture, a torture so horrible that I am ashamed of ever showing myself. It is that which might make me decide to stay at home. At eight o'clock, Dr. D. found my general condition much better, but what can he do against this lace of nerves which defend themselves by such revolt?

I have shot the memorable scene of Marais slapping Mila. I expected to do only one take, but Michel, put off by the slap, forgot his part. Five minutes earlier, poor Mila, who is always having odd experiences, was hurrying to her dressing room when she caught her foot in her dress, fell and got a large bruise on her right cheek. We finally got a good take. Mila sobbed and Marais comforted her; the dressers rushed round her and made up for the necessity to keep silent while we were recording the slap.

---

[38] [Ferdinand Roybet (1840–1920), French painter.]

Tuesday the 23rd.

Lymphangitis. Phlegmon on the neck. Impetigo starting again. Bronchitis. Did yesterday's scene again this morning. Beauty's room. Decided with Paulvé and Darbon to stop the film.

Wednesday, noon.

Can't bear the agony of my face any more. This morning Paul went to see Professor Martin to get me admitted into the Pasteur Institute. I have an appointment there at 2:30. I am in such pain I even wonder if I can hold out till then. I am terribly distressed at having to interrupt the work. But I have stood all I can. I can't bear any more. It's driving me mad.

Thursday the 25th.

I am reminded of what Thomas Mann wrote to me a long time ago when I was at Toulon with typhoid: "Your type dies in a hospital."

I've been here in the Pasteur Institute since yesterday. Professor Martin was kind enough to let me have a bed straight away. (The door of his apartment house opens out under the archway of the Institute.) Marais saw me into my cell, then went home to get linen, butter, fruit, cigarettes and the notebook and pencil I'm now using. They started the penicillin treatment immediately. Penicillin and the atom bomb are now the height of fashion. But like all fashions, they will pass. The word "penicillin" will, to those who read these notes one day, produce the same effect as the word "panorama" in *Père Goriot*. The atom bomb will become just a squib.

But in 1945, penicillin produces extraordinary cures. I'm injected every three hours. The very painful injection is the one in the morning in the hard but sensitive core of the carbuncles. They can't do anything for the impetigo and dermatitis on my face until my neck's better. A hospital is the only serious nursing home. I am in a sort of small surgical ward, where the doctors and nurses want nothing better than to get you well quickly. If a visitor comes he can only see me through the glass. I haven't any books. I won't write anything here but these notes. I won't let myself think about the film. This is a breathing spell, a parenthesis of calm. — Shut up at Saint-Maurice, blinded by pain, I didn't even realize it was autumn. From my iron bed I can see an old brick wall through the French windows, and some trees losing their yellow leaves as they're blown by the wind.

5 o'clock.

Jeannot, Paul, Michel Auclair came to see me. They were allowed into my ward, but I'm afraid people may find out who I am. The last thing I want is to have special favors. I'm in a hospital and would like it to remain a hospital. An occasional visit to break this astonishing solitude then becomes something wonderful. When I saw Michel's good face outside my window my heart jumped with pleasure. Josette and Nane are to come tomorrow.

I thought Jeannot looked off color and he's got a cough. I made him promise to go and see Martin, and get an appointment. He did so and has one for tomorrow at eleven o'clock.

I have just eaten the bowl of soup and the carrots that reappear every day. That's perfect too. You can picture the magical role of the fruit or champagne people bring us. It's like Beauty coming into the wash-house dressed as a princess.

Friday, October 26, 1945.

I had terrible itching this morning, particularly on the lower part of my face. On the other hand, my neck and shoulders don't trouble me so much. It seems that those very painful injections of penicillin into the carbuncles have stopped the lymphangitis which looked as if it might become a phlegmon.

Penicillin is only active for three hours. That's why the patient has to be injected constantly. When the means is found to stabilize its effects, the germs will have armed themselves against it, and the genius which the species deploys to defend itself will triumph over man again. What makes one think of man in relation to germs is that they both defend themselves by destroying the place that they occupy.

The doctors came. Martin is stopping the general penicillin treatment, and I'm only to have the hateful injections. However, these do seem to get immediate results.

The Merchant's home.
The arrow lands in the
sisters' room (p.66).

Hammond Collection

The Merchant's home.
The sisters in Beauty's
room (p. 83).

Hammond Collection

Professor Aubin came to see me. He's an excellent fellow. When Jean Marais had otitis, he used to come every day to the Place de la Madeleine. He'd never accept a penny. (It was just the same with Martin, who was Marais's general practitioner at about the same time, and then certainly not as well off as he is today.)

Marais became so friendly with them that he's always talking about them. He used to say he would have liked to have Aubin for a father. He would let him puncture his ears again and again, and never flinch, and he'd never have an anesthetic.

My secretary is being phoned all day long: "We hear that Cocteau has a beard. Can we photograph him?" The stoicism of reporters: perfect indifference to other people's suffering.

The doctor has just given me a local injection. It was terrible. I feel that he really doesn't like to inflict such agony although he must be used to it by now.

I wonder what Jean-Pierre Aumont would think if he could see me in this glass cage, being cured by America (penicillin) and fed by the butter in the packages he sends me from Hollywood.

Saturday morning the 27th, 10 o'clock.

My face itched again during the night, and my right hand, which had begun to clear up, tormented me and suppurated slightly. The doctor came to administer the penicillin torture while the insurance company's doctor looked on. It has been decided that I shall stay in the hospital till next Wednesday, and shall then still need four or five days off. I hope to start work again on that Tuesday or Wednesday at Saint-Maurice.

The psychology of these nuns is interesting. They're not supposed to show their kind feelings, so that they become automata of kindness. It is as impossible for them to reveal their own personality as it is for many actors to make a movement on the stage which they haven't rehearsed—for instance, when somebody's hat accidentally falls off, they can't even pick it up. These excellent nuns nurse the patient's ward. They do not nurse the patient. His case is too individual. That would require initiative. Initiative would upset the routine and in their eyes amount to treason against the head doctor. The patient is in pain during the night? He must wait the rounds. Then in comes an automaton, draped in linen, who tidies the cell and disappears again. Which doesn't prevent these nurses from being charming, gay and ready to laugh at any little thing.

The whole Pasteur Institute is organized round contagious diseases. No exception can be made without disastrous effects. The result is that patients like myself, who are being treated with penicillin but are not themselves contagious, have to follow the same rules as those who are. We cannot open or shut the transoms, cross the threshold of the room, or drink or eat without having our plate or mug taken away by a sort of a murderer's glove stained with blood.

These figures of Lady Macbeth, ghosts draped in white linen with red gloves, come and go through the corridors with arms extended, like Josette going through the wall to her father, thanks to the blue glove.

2 o'clock.

Paul's just gone off with the Swiss publishers and Gaston Bonheur.[39] They were allowed in without any questions asked. I have signed the contract for my complete works and they're going back to Geneva this evening.

Sunday the 28th.

This morning, while I was pondering about the incredible number of odd things still left for us to do, such as some work with sound to link up and strengthen some of the visuals, and was in general meditating on the care and patience which go into any film, it occurred to me how pathetic it is that French audiences are in general so grossly inattentive and indifferent both to the cinema and the stage. They are seldom hypnotized by the screen, except for the working-class viewers, *the only ones who listen and look*. The great gentlemen and ladies fidget, shuffle for a cigarette in the dark, can't find one, turn round and ask somebody behind for one, light it, put it out, from time to time accidentally catch some image which ceased to have any meaning (but what do they care, they are only interested in criticizing someone's profile and somebody's dress). It seems to me that this crime of inattention, which no one admits to, is the worst crime against art, and contributes to the general

---

[39] [Writer of plays, novels and biographies.]

disintegration of intelligence.

Egoism is at the bottom of such conduct. "I reach the theater, I look for my seat, I disturb the audience and the actors, I despise the play; so what—other people don't exist or exist only in so far as they can satisfy my pleasure." Odd pleasure! Every work of art is incomprehensible if we skip a single line. And yet this public which judges, which dares to judge, arrives at the end of the first act.

That's why gradually this incorrigible public ends up getting the gruel it deserves and which it can enjoy without thinking.

What universes such imbeciles miss! If they only knew what waves of sustenance can flow between a theatrical performance and an eye and ear that don't want to miss any of it, their lives would perhaps cease to be such whirlpools of vacuity.

Perhaps there ought to be a Conservatoire for audiences. But, unfortunately, if it's like the one for performers, they would learn nothing. It would merely produce an even wider rift between the stage and the audience.

France, it seems, is the only country in Europe where such filthy manners are prevalent. In China, Indo-China and Japan the theater is, of course, a cult; but I was thinking of England and Germany, where I have been to the theater and noticed that any member of the audience who crumpled a cigarette paper would find himself before a tribunal of disapproving eyes.

In France, we started off by thinking kindness is a form of stupidity and unkindness a form of intelligence. Nowadays politeness is considered a waste of time. I gather proof of this every day.

I stood aside to allow a lady to get out of the Métro. "You're blocking the door deliberately!" she screamed. This lady was red with hatred.

I have a habit of saying "Thank you" to the women who punch my ticket. Many think that I am making fun of them and shrug their shoulders with disgust.

I'm beginning to see the sense of the nuns' admirable routine, and realize that any individualistic deviation would take the starch out of the coifs which frame their faces and which keep them moving straight ahead from minute to minute, from week to week, from year to year, like a plough-horse.

It's extremely difficult for a very free spirit to put himself in the place of one of these cogs in a machine, these grains of sand. They could reply, "You are also a cog." And that is perfectly true.

Martin came. He thinks the wounds are going on all right. The carbuncle on my neck is still firm. The rest is improving. He's left off the martyrdom for Sunday. Even when I've left the Pasteur Institute, cured, I shall have to start work with bandages still on.

Sunday evening, 7 o'clock.

Now night is falling, the strange hospital night with its huge silence after many visitors. My cell is a high blue and white kitchen, rocked like a ship's cabin by the movie the shadows make on the walls. This play of shadows, like watered silk or the marble ceilings of a seaside hotel, is complicated by the cells on each side, the windows, the corridor, and the windows of apartment houses behind the trees.

Waves of friends have left caviar, flowers and bottles of champagne. This doesn't at all match the style of my kitchen, and makes it look like a kitchen in an American film.

It's raining. Nane tells me that the insurance companies don't regard me as a good risk and are not keen on covering me for another film. All right. I'll write books. I'll produce plays. I'll leave behind me a report on existence with *La Belle* as I did with *Le Sang d'un Poète*.

Of course, if the insurance companies realized how you burn yourself out in such undertakings, they'd never insure any of our breed and would only cover gilt-edged productions. Clément, who came to see me with Bella, says that Saint-Maurice is sinister and empty. Work on *Le Collier de la Reine*[40] is still interrupted by crises with the producers. Our sets are ready. The studio hands are idle. I hope to God that I can get on my feet soon.

10 o'clock.

This is the hour when the man coughs. His cough sometimes

---

[40] [*L'Affaire du Collier de la Reine* (1946), directed by Marcel L'Herbier.]

wakes me with a jolt. It's terrifying. It emerges, swells, forms scrolls and excrescences till it's like a lacerated orchid. It becomes fabulous like the voice of the Minotaur in the corridors of the labyrinth, innumerable like the clouds of explosives in a war film. He's been in this hospital a year. If it weren't for him it would be a rest cure here; but with him it's hell. One just waits from cough to cough.

Monday the 29th.

And now I must tell the truth. I have never been so happy as I have since I've been ill. The pain's nothing. I've pulled through thanks to my unit's kindness, graciousness and affection. I am receiving my reward for having chosen them. The never-ending obligation to give a good example and stay on my feet was almost exalting. My suffering was a contribution to the film and I'm sure it hasn't been for nothing. I gave in only when I saw I was no longer giving it anything but death.

I suppose it's only right and just that my face should be spoiled, should swell, crack, be covered with sores and hair, and that my hands should bleed and erupt, since I am covering Marais's face and hand with a shell so painful that the removal of his makeup resembles the agony of my dressings. All of this corresponds to a certain spiritual style that is mine. If it were otherwise, I'd be quite worried.

Emile Darbon came to see me in very good form and full of that good advice which reassures me. It is evident that Darbon likes the film and the unit, and is bored without us. — I told him what I had been told about the insurance, and he shrugged his shoulders.

Saw Martin. It is clear that the trouble I was having on my forehead and am having between the fingers of my right hand are beyond his powers. He advises me to see the specialists at Saint-Louis.

When the doctor came this morning, the root of the carbuncle came out. Its size amazed me. The doctor said: "You've a hole as big as a franc in the nape of your neck."

Dr. Dumas came. He's cross because I can't go and recuperate up in the mountains before starting work on the film again. He said: "What a lot of flies in your room! Pasteur hated them."

10 p.m.

Many visitors. I was brought champagne, chicken, flowers, cigarettes. My little kitchen is too small to hold all the presents. Alekan informs me that we are going to get 6,000 metres of Agfa stock. He's in despair after seeing the day-before-yesterday's rushes, as he now realizes that all the work we've done would be a hundred times more effective if we had had really sensitive film. I'll keep this good stock for the dark hall in the Beast's castle. Darbon didn't say anything about it to me this morning but I hear he hopes to get a bit more.

Alekan tells me that all the material I think is admirable is considered by some people at the studio as hopeless, badly lit, white cheese. Doesn't he know yet what I have been used to for years?—every time anybody tries anything out of the ordinary, people go blind and can see only what looks like things they've already seen. People have decided once and for all that fuzziness is poetic. Now, since in my eyes poetry is precision, number, I'm pushing Alekan in precisely the opposite direction from what fools think is poetic. He is slightly bewildered. He does not yet have my long acquaintance with struggle, my serenity in the face of the follies of the age.

Nothing seems so dreary to me as the photographic uniformity of a film which the know-alls call style. A film must distract the eye with its contrasts, with effects which attempt, not to copy those of nature, but to find that truth which Goethe contrasts with reality (Rubens's engravings of sheep, which Goethe showed to Eckermann, where the shadow is on the same side as the sun). Sometimes I light one face more than another, light a room more or less strongly than it would be naturally, or give a candle the power of a lamp. In the Beast's park I use a sort of twilight which doesn't correspond to the time of day when Beauty goes out. If it suits my purpose, I will link up this twilight with moonlight. And it's not just because I'm dealing with a fairy story that I treat realism in such a high-handed way. A film is a piece of writing in pictures, and I try to give it an atmosphere which will bring out the feeling in the film rather than correspond to the facts.

Tuesday the 30th.

The doctor thinks I ought to stay over Thursday, and perhaps

Friday too.

I'm afraid these sulphanilamide dressings may bring my face out in nettle-rash again, as the skin's so sensitive. It would be better if I came back to the Institute and had my penicillin dressings here. But I don't see how I can, as the studio hours don't fit with the Institute's.

Yesterday, somebody brought in the *Grand Ecart* manuscript (though I don't know who owns it). I didn't recognize it because the school exercise books have been stuck onto pages and numbered, and the whole sumptuously bound. Suddenly, on turning over a sheet which contained only the cover of the pale green notebook, decorated with a rooster and scrawled with doodles, I saw again the hotel at Le Lavandou, the Pension Bessy at Pramousquier and Radiguet rolling his cigarettes and taking notes for *Le Bal du Comte d'Orgel*. I was overcome with nostalgia.[41]

Tuesday evening.

Here I am alone with the coughing man and the interplay of shadows. The dressing has stuck to my neck and hurts, but I can't get anyone to come. Not only do the time-honored customs of the Pasteur Institute prescribe calling people by tapping a spoon against a cup, which no one can hear; there's practically no one there anyway between seven and eleven of an evening. — Marcel Jouhandeau[42] left about seven. He'd been telling me some sort of fairy stories about rams, cocks and chicks.

A very charming nun has just been in and given me a fresh dressing. Aldo brought me the new stills to choose and Budry brought the large photos he's keeping for *Formes et Couleurs,* so I could write the captions. He'll come for them tomorrow.

Many people, many presents again. My little cell is full of things which I can't share with the other patients as it's against the hospital rules. I can't bear to see them all wasted and I invent dodges which make it possible for my neighbors in other rooms to enjoy some too.

[41][Cocteau wrote his first two novels, *Le Grand Ecart* (highly autobiographical) and *Thomas l'Imposteur,* in 1922 (both published the following year) while at Le Lavandou (on the Mediterranean between Saint Tropez and Toulon) and Pramousquier with his young protégé Raymond Radiguet, who during the same months was correcting the proofs of his first novel, *Le Diable au Corps,* and starting his second, *Le Bal du Comte d'Orgel.*]

[42][Distinguished French novelist, born 1888.]

Wednesday morning.

Almost all night and this morning I read the book which Jouhandeau brought me yesterday. There are only four copies so far. *Essai sur moi-même.* As I closed the book last night, I thought of the remark Roger Lannes quotes from *Le Potomak* :[43] "God made man in his own image. Tempted by God as others are by the devil, I press myself to myself with all my strength."

Jouhandeau's book is a book of love. It should be called *Tristan and Tristan.* It's already acquired a "halo" and Marcel can afford to laugh at the conspiracy of silence that is being organized against him.

He tells me he has regained his balance ever since he's taken to getting up at four in the morning to work. No one in the world disturbs him, everyone's asleep. He escapes from the whirlpool of men. When the others stir, he has finished his work.

Wednesday evening, 10 o'clock.

How can I protect my silence? How can I prevent this noise that arises spontaneously round my silence? How can I stop these write-ups, photographs and all the fantastic rumors which ruin my silence and prevent me from getting on calmly with my work? I have an inexplicable fate, an unhappy faculty of gathering crowds which raise around me that hubbub I detest and which the journalists increase every day in all good faith, a misplaced kindness against which I am helpless. Shall I always have to put up with either extreme fulsome praise or personal insults, and be the center of a legend that devours me and won't allow my work to develop in peace?

November 2, 1945.

I came back to the Palais-Royal yesterday evening. Paul and Jeannot fetched me in a car from the Institute. I thought I was quite strong. As soon as I got outside I found I was unsteady on my legs. There was an absolute mountain of letters at my flat. Unfortunately, I can't answer them. I couldn't write a line yesterday evening. I am resuming this diary today, Friday, 2 p.m. The barber's just shaved me. He'll be back about six to wash and cut my hair. — The

---

[43] [Book by Cocteau (written in 1913–14, first published 1919, definitive edition 1924), the earliest of his works not disowned as juvenilia.]

insurance company wanted me to work tomorrow. They must be crazy. I'll try and start filming again on Tuesday, though the doctors at the Institute prescribed two weeks in the country for a change of air. The main thing is to hold out.

November 3, 1945.

Telephone calls from agents, the company, the insurance people. The doctor came and said: "Only one thing can cure you altogether and quickly: a month in the mountains. If that's impossible, two or three days or even a week wouldn't do any good. You might just as well start work on the day you have arranged." There I agree with him. So I will let the unit get things rolling again on Monday with Marcel André and Josette (odd shots which I need for the editing). I shall go back to Saint-Maurice on Tuesday and start on Beauty's room.

Since this morning I've been answering the phone, walking in the Palais-Royal, standing up among my innumerable visitors and exhausting myself deliberately to see how my strength holds out. I got through to eight o'clock (when I dined across the street) without fatigue. Certainly, my face still itches but I believe that's only because the skin's healing and not due to any new trouble. I may be mistaken and may find out so at Joinville. I shall risk the experiment, whatever the cost. It's one thing to fall back on the insurance, but quite another to leave all these people in the lurch.

Ibéria came this morning. She says she is going to look after me and make me stay seated, which I normally never do. The doctor will watch me and I will watch my diet. I must not fall a victim to worry and the fear of a relapse. As I can't have the mountain air, I shall have to find some inner freshness.

I have just remembered something strange. Fate was trying to stop our trip to the Bassin d'Arcachon. Everything got in our way, impeded us and counseled us against leaving. I stubbornly ignored the omens. I accepted General Corniglion's offer of his plane. The pilot nearly killed us all at La Rochelle. Fate was arranging its obstacles. After a day of waiting in a wasteland infested with mosquitoes and diphtheria, the camp commandant, discouraged, found us a car in which we proceeded to the port with one breakdown after another. I came to think we would be blown up by a mine.

It wasn't a mine that threatened us, and from which fate was trying to keep me; it was sunburn and the fatal mosquitoes of that grey pearl, the inlet, surrounded by garbage cans—the fishermen empty their filth behind their huts. The miseries that now overwhelm me started there.

Monday the 5th, 11 a.m.

Far too many people yesterday. Stroll in the Palais-Royal. Tired out. At five o'clock the nettle-rash flared up on my face again and my eyes swelled. Darbon telephoned from Joinville this morning. I have made them start again without me (Marcel André in the mist; Josette's faint). I gave precise instructions to Ibéria, Clément and Lucile yesterday evening. Clément brought me the negative of the stag. It isn't bad to the eye. I will see what it's like on the screen. Radio Monte-Carlo came to my room ten minutes ago to record an interview about the film.

Monday evening.

Clément phones me as they go along from shot to shot. Aramis without his groom kicked and plunged and smashed the set. Josette won't ride him.

My nettle-rash wasn't so bad today. Darbon is worried because I'm starting work again *but I'm determined to start tomorrow.* The car is to fetch me at 8:30.

Tuesday the 6th, 8 a.m.

Colette,[44] whom I dropped in on yesterday, is suffering from lumbago. She told me of an article in an American scientific magazine brought by the Polignacs. In it the American scientists apologize for letting loose carbuncles and skin diseases over the whole face of the globe as a direct result of their atomic researches. Perhaps I am a victim of this research, as I was a victim years ago, when I fell in the rue d'Anjou at the same time as the tidal wave in Japan, which Claudel[45] recounted to me afterwards.

[44][The noted author (1873-1954) was a neighbor of Cocteau's in the Palais-Royal section of Paris.]

[45] [The poet-playwright-diplomat Paul Claudel (1868-1955) was France's ambassador to Japan at the time of the great earthquake and tidal wave in 1924.]

I am to work again on the film. I am as excited as a child at Christmas. I woke up too early, got up too early; I couldn't keep still at all.

Tuesday, 10 p.m.

I felt very happy and excited going to Saint-Maurice again. Nothing is finer than writing a poem with people, faces, hands, lights, objects, all of which you can put exactly where you want them. The whole unit fêted me. They brought me armchairs and blankets. I worked easily and seriously. I found the right movements for the actresses and the camera without much difficulty. The actresses obeyed the slightest pressure from the invisible thread I held between my fingers. We were doing the continuation of Beauty's room. Seated at her dressing-table, she has just put on her grand court dress, her crown and her veil, in order to believe in her dream. She looks at herself in a small mirror. She is bathed in a supernatural light, which fades as she turns round, hearing the latch lift on the door. Her sisters come in. They throw the mirror on the bed, and go out. Beauty rises, takes up the mirror, presses her cheek sensuously against it, props it up against the candlesticks, and lies down beside this proof of her adventure. Before I did this scene, I had previously done the one in which the sisters, having just rubbed their eyes with onions, sob and beg her not to go away again.

At noon I saw the run-through of the deer. One shot in which the reclining animal, camouflaged by mimicry, dappled like the leaves, springs up and bounds away, has come off marvelously.

At 6:30 I saw yesterday's rushes which Clément described to me over the phone when they were being shot. Marcel André in the mist. Josette's cry as she first sees the Beast, and faints. I also saw the difference between the Kodak test and the Agfa test. It's enormous.

My nettle-rash has almost cleared up. The cure has begun.

Wednesday the 7th, 7:30 a.m.

Marais left at 7:30 to make up for the scene of the Beast weeping in the magic mirror. Last night my eye swelled and wrinkled. The car is to fetch me at 8:30. I wish I could finish Beauty's room.

I would go on to the great hall, and then to the sisters' room.

At Saint-Maurice Beauty's bed-curtains have been stolen. I have replaced them with the ones from the sisters' room.

Wednesday the 7th, 10 p.m.

I haven't got nettle-rash after all. It's eczema, a tenacious and mysterious thing. The doctor is trying new injections but unfortunately he's concluded that because my whole system is so run-down, I'm now a prey to every illness. My teeth are giving me trouble. And I haven't a single minute to get to the dentist. It's terrible to be so young and yet so old. What an imbalance!

From nine o'clock this morning till seven this evening I worked on the special effects in Beauty's room. The trick with the mirrors, making them reflect two people at once one after the other (Josette and Jeannot), the trick of the mirror breaking—Josette's disappearances and appearances. The studio hands worked furiously, constructing, demolishing, driving nails in and pulling nails out. Whenever I'm in the projection room I can't help wondering how brilliant and fresh scenes can ever come out of the places—covered in dust and cold as cellars—where we work. To live in a dream world at Saint-Maurice, then go home and sleep in earnest—that's the rhythm I like. But I'm always terrified of waking up with some new signal of pain.

Thursday the 8th, 10 p.m.

Dr. D. came to the studio to watch me filming and discovered that most of the trouble on my face is due to artificial sunburn caused by the arcs. Which doesn't surprise me, for I had the same red bags under my left eye eight years ago after extended exposure to the sun on the water at Samois.

When studio hands get the same trouble they treat it by rubbing grated raw potato on their faces. It was raining. I shot the scenes with the important guests in the main hall of the Merchant's house. Escoffier grouped them round the table very well, in "Anatomy Lesson" fashion.[46] A shot of the father's entrance with the guests, as seen by Beauty from the sisters' room. And the one of the entrance which precedes it, taken from the top of the banisters, between the

[46] [Refers to Rembrandt's painting *The Anatomy Lesson of Professor Nicolaes Tulp* (1632).]

The Merchant's home.
The sisters on their way
to visit the Duchess.

The Merchant's home. The important guests in the main hall (p. 84).

Hammond Collection

loggia and the staircase. This afternoon I ran what would have been five shots into one big one. It makes it difficult for Tiquet but whenever it's possible I like those broad movements with the camera rushing from one character to the other.

I'd hoped to finish. At 7:30 I was still at it and Marcel André had to run off to his theater. Only one shot left to do. I will do it tomorrow morning. (Tiresome day. The draper in the closet.)

Friday the 9th, 7 a.m.

My left eye has swollen up considerably during the night. Yesterday Faguet, Mila's doctor, took some tests from the scabs on my hand and forehead, to examine them at the Institute and see whether they aren't fungus which only iodine can destroy.

Dr. Dumas and his wife were astonished and overwhelmed by Saint-Maurice. People who have never been to such strange places are astonished at this tumult, these scaffoldings put up in five minutes and topped with rails, these ghostly sets arranged to suit camera angles (the rest of the space filled up with people and wraps), these lights which seem to cancel each other out, but end up on the screen as ordinary sunlight or moonlight.

The dresses are getting crumpled, torn and frayed, but they *come alive*. At first an actress hardly dares move in them. Later, used to them, she finds she can move with ease in the heaviest sleeves, the stiffest collar and the longest train. The details which worry the dressers and the continuity girl so much don't matter on the screen. I never hesitate to shift the furniture around, either. It's difficult enough in ordinary life to remember where a thing was precisely. Even more in pictures. I chose the takes of the forest. The general effect is remarkable, in the style of Perrault. It's important to wait before selecting. The day after shooting, you are still overcome by what you have seen, you notice nothing but the mistakes, you are hypnotized by absurd details.

The wonderful thing about films is this perpetual card trick done in front of the audience without letting them see how it's done.

Nature has given us nerves for suffering and warning, and an intelligence for knowing how to suffer and for keeping on guard. The struggle against suffering interests me as much as the work on the film.

Saturday, 9 p.m.

I won't say "what fine work" (I don't know if it was), but: what good hard work I've done since yesterday morning. Everything came easily and fell unexpectedly into place. My eye didn't bother me; I didn't feel tired. Actors, cameramen, workmen, were all lifted by a single wing which seemed to come from my heart. We were doing the comic scene where Marais and Auclair mimic the sisters in the great hall after they've shut the draper up in a closet. First of all I did the shots of the draper in the dark, illuminating an eye, his nose or his mouth with just a crack of light. I tackled the Ludovic–Avenant farce this morning. I built a vertical rail from the ground to the loggia so that the camera could follow them up and down. After lunch (I had lunch with Bérard, Boris, Marie-Louise Bousquet and an American journalist) I demolished the rail and put another up in such a way that when the camera reached the end, it could turn and take the whole room in one sweep. With this gadget I was able to shoot the boys' sequence in one go, when they mimic their sisters, snatching up a tapestry to use as a train; in short, I prepared to perfection for the dubbing of Mila's and Nane's voices when the boys are imitating them. This way I telescoped what would have been a dozen shots into four. I hadn't time for the last shot. So I shot eleven. I'll do the twelfth on Monday morning before going upstairs to the sisters' room.

Monday the 12th, 8 a.m.

Spent Sunday mentally correcting the editing of the opening of the film. In my opinion the cinema should play around with time and space. There is no need for the arrow shot to take place within a realistic time. I will show the dog on the cushion before the arrow lands, as if the audience were in the room a little before the dispatching of the arrow which they have seen leaving the bow. I'll dwell longer on Jeannot's hand after he's been pushed and a split second more on Nane climbing on the chair. Claude's first montage is too realistic, too far from a personal handwriting. Example: In Hugo, Claude Frollo is pushed from the top of Notre-Dame by Quasimodo. Another chapter begins: "Falls from such heights are rarely perpendicular. The archdeacon . . . ." Let's hope we have some luck this afternoon! I'd like to make the scene where the faces of Beauty and Avenant appear a very beautiful one. So far in the film they've only been seen from behind.

Monday evening, 10 o'clock.

Harmonious work. The shooting script, the dream, the prerequisite imagination, the lights, the room, the linen hanging in front of the fireplace, the artists—everything was smooth, easy, in place.

Run-through of the important guests' scene and the first day of the draper farce. It was authentically personal handwriting, not screened through any filter. The mistakes don't matter much. They put things in relief. It was as if I were *looking at* Mozart music. (That music in which the slightest detail—four notes—can stand out well in isolation, and the whole movement is entirely admirable.) Visually—so far—it resembles the *Magic Flute* overture.

Tuesday the 13th, 7 a.m.

I tried to eat some fish and was taken ill immediately. My eyes puffed up again and the irritation returned. Terrible itching. Dr. N. had told me: "Thanks to Antergan you can eat whatever you fancy."

Money, an ill-starred thing, becomes a lucky star in the workings of a film. For only the fear of losing it drives the producers to give us what we need with such alacrity, exactitude and cooperation. The car would be hours late when it fetched us, the workmen would fritter their time away, sets would remain half-built, hard-to-find objects would not fly into our hands of their own volition.

I am writing this while waiting for the car. The current's gone off. I am using the light of a candle. These blackouts put us behind. The actors can't make up. My schedule will be all behind by the time I get there. Furthermore, blackouts could mean disaster in the lab.

For five years I've been knotted up, paralyzed by a hostile, hateful, dangerous atmosphere. My gift of being able to improvise in front of an audience left me completely. But I find gradually that I can relax again. Sometimes I can think about some problem and solve it in words, alone in my room. Perhaps I'll regain that pleasant contact with the public. I wonder if I shall?

Raising my eyes (I have my notebook on my knee), I've just caught sight of one of those accidental effects which happen now and then, and which my work obliges me to achieve constantly. The candle reflected in the glass covering the Antinoe[47] mask makes its left temple look curled and hollowed out, as if it were an extension, in the form of a white wound, of the curls of the hair and beard. The flame is very high and seems to come from the very center of its spirit. The enamel eyes shine and reflect this straight flame which burns behind them. There is something divine in this optical phenomenon.

I spent two hours yesterday arranging the shot in which Josette sees her reflection in the floor she's polishing, where Jeannot's hand comes into the picture to retrieve the arrow.

To reorganize chance. That's the basis of our work.

Tuesday evening, 10 o'clock.

I'm disfigured, devoured by these rashes swelling my eyes and cheeks. All I ask is to be able to go on working with people who accept me as I am and like me. This morning I telescoped six shots into one, thanks to Tiquet's suppleness and precision with his camera; anybody would think it had wings and could go up or down, plunge, pause, come to rest anywhere he likes. (Jeannot, Josette and Michel's scenes in the sisters' room.) People who watch a film being shot for the first time are astonished at the chaos, at all the clutter littered over the set, at a scene begun over and over again and taking place only a few inches from a crowd of workmen and spotlight stands. But once projected, this scene is isolated, and starts to live in a vacuum where every detail is thrown into relief and the smallest fault appears monstrous. This afternoon we filmed, downstairs, the chess and usurer scene—the men removing the furniture. As soon as the film gets away from the leading characters and an alien element is introduced, the rhythm is broken and it requires an incredible effort to get it back again. Sometimes I arrange a scene from one angle and direct it from a place that has nothing to do with the camera angle. From 2:30 to 6:30 I was on a high gallery, similar to the one at the Hôtel de Bourgogne,

[47][Ancient Egyptian city founded by the Emperor Hadrian c. 130 A.D. in memory of his favorite, Antinous; the city became a center of Greco-Roman culture.]

The Merchant's home. Avenant retrieves the arrow as Beauty polishes the floor (p. 88).

Hammond Collection

The Merchant's home.
The chess and usurer
scene (p. 88).

Hammond Collection

watching the countless errors of the Russian actor who's playing the usurer. He couldn't move or talk. He looked the part perfectly, but for the rest he was absolutely hopeless. If these shots of him screen as badly as they played, I'll double the part myself. Courage. Courage. Courage.

Thursday evening, 11 o'clock.

Couldn't write yesterday. I was too exhausted by the work and a late run-through. Alekan's improved enormously with the actors and the study of their faces. As the takes we shot first will come after the others and he will be at his best at the end of the job (which will also be the end of the film), perhaps these differences in quality which I notice won't be conspicuous. The current went off seven times today. Practically nothing was done. And nothing is more demoralizing than that Saint-Maurice factory when everything is turned off and cold, with only a few workmen holding out on the sets by candlelight.

Berard, with the property men (and entirely by candlelight), designed and cut out the covering of the stone Diana who shoots an arrow and kills Avenant, and he draped it over some young woman he's discovered. I finished the great hall. I have still got a shot to do in the sisters' room, from another angle. (Josette Day is laid up with gastric flu and confined to her room for a week, so I shall have to do something else.) Tomorrow I shall go on to the skylight of Diana's pavilion. It looks like an absolute conservatory of ivy, snow and glass.

Saturday evening the 17th, 11 o'clock.

How many different things I've learned in these last two days which have been so busy that I couldn't find time to write!

I did the shot of the boys arriving at the pavilion of Diana (taken from below and above). I began the high shots seen from inside this square tower, which is covered with white ivy and dark ivy inside. Without doubt this tricky set is one of Bérard's most wonderful conceptions.

Here is the way I get this man, who flames with disorder and the precision of a maniac, to work: I anticipate him. I show him a mediocre set. He gets upset, gets excited, alters it, metamorphoses it until it matches my dream. The exterior of the pavilion surpasses by far what I expected. It is pure Gustave Doré illustrating Perrault (for example, the Prince arriving at Sleeping Beauty's castle). On the roof, when the boys climb the iron ladder and come out into the open, it is just like that. The glass shines like a diamond. The ivy covering it throws sharp shadows on the people who move along it. On the right, an architecture of globes and acanthus recalls the Raray walls. The part I am filming comes near the end of the film, and I still have half the film, or nearly half, to shoot. Between four and five o'clock, Avenant had already been pierced by Diana's white arrow (Diana won't be filmed until Monday). Marais was hanging in space, holding on to Ludovic's hands. It was an enormous effort to keep this pose. An archer on a platform aimed at his back, which was protected by a mail shirt and a cork pad underneath his cape. The archer was shooting straight ahead. He refused to shoot up at an angle, fearing an accident. Marais insisted. He let fly. The arrow glanced off, slid over the cloth, and grazed the back of Marais's neck. The archer said: "I might pierce his neck."

I refused to do another take. But Marais then found a way of sloping his back toward us and this time the arrow planted itself in the exact position. At every attempt those present had a jolt, convinced that they'd see Marais killed by the arrow. In the previous shot he was supposed to break the glass panes and the frame with a kick, thrust his bow impatiently through the last pane, and speak when the hole was completed. The first time, the frame didn't break enough. The second time, it flew at the camera. The third time, Marais forgot his lines. The fourth time was all right. After each bad attempt, the property men had to put back the frame, put new glass in it, and nail up the ivy branches again. Because of these endless attempts for a short scene I was able to shoot only four numbers. I had to stop at the close-up of the hands changing into the Beast's, as Ludovic lets him fall.

Monday, noon to eight. In the morning Bérard will prepare the statue of Diana, the snow-covered floor, the treasures. Diana's bow will not have a string. She will handle the arrow as if she were tensing the bow. She won't be seen shooting. The arrow will be seen piercing Avenant's back (which we've already taken). This will be followed by his fall in the snow (with the Beast's face and hands).

Have seen some rough cuts of the editing. This is an awkward stage. For I am accustomed to seeing the same takes four or five times consecutively, with all the details and the delays of the apparatus, and now, in a cut copy, everything seems strange to me and the film seems to be moving too quickly. I must get used to this stage in the work and find the slowness in what seems so brief. To do this I must wait till I can see more objectively, when I've forgotten all the personal associations which are attached to each frame. When the film's shot, Ibéria, Jacques Lebreton and I will have an overwhelming job doing the mixings.

Haven't seen any rushes these last few days. The lab doesn't dare to do developing because the electricity is so frequently being cut off. I tremble at the possibility of a catastrophe which would compel me to do again that which can't be done again.

Monday the 19th, 11 p.m.

Yesterday, Sunday, I was forced into a car to see Dejobert about the lithographs which I am never able to finish (the *Deux Travestis: Fantôme de Marseille* and the *Numéro Barbette*).[48] I got on so quickly that I had finished my stone before D.'s son had done the frames. I wanted to get home and go to bed. But out of luck. Friends came in and it's the only day I can see them.

I got to the studio at 10:30 this morning. Bérard was working on the snow set and on Doudou's make-up. She is a Creole. She loathes cold weather. I don't blame her. I had decided to do the same thing for Diana that I did in *Le Sang d'un Poète*: dress the actress at the last minute with anything that came to hand. But unfortunately, it's difficult to do that in a full-scale film. Alekan was worried about the lighting in this set, which is closed in, high, and doesn't permit moving back. To allow Ara to go on with the make-up I insisted on doing a big close-up of Michel looking frightened to match up with Avenant's transformation into the Beast.

They led Doudou onto the set as she couldn't see; her own eyes were covered by the statue's false ones. Carrier was carrying her. She was freezing. She had gooseflesh. They warmed her up with

48[These lithographs were to illustrate the book *Deux Travestis* (published 1947), consisting of two short literary works: the story *Le Fantôme de Marseille* (original publication 1933; later reworked as a dramatic monologue for Edith Piaf), about a handsome burglar who masquerades as a woman while "on the lam"; and *Le Numéro Barbette* ("Barbette" was a tightrope walker named Van der Clyde who impersonated a woman in his Parisian music-hall act in the 1920's).]

lamps. Alekan hesitated, experimented, tried to make the treasure shine. Doudou hadn't got to bed till seven in the morning. She had no idea what discipline film work requires. She just avoided a fit of hysterics. She was half asleep.

We got the gear into position using a stand-in draped in linen. Finally, when we were ready to shoot, Doudou was carried onto her pedestal. The resistors exploded and flames shot out. Doudou refused to get off her pedestal. We made her comfortable with cushions. I was afraid she would faint. Bérard lost his head and shouted. The repair job was undertaken. I climbed the ladder fifty times. The resistors repaired, we resumed shooting. The down which we were using for snow grazed poor Diana and stuck to her blind eyes.

After that take I said to myself: "That's it. She won't work any more. She'll just walk out on us." But she seemed to be more encouraged. We left the heights. We set up the camera rails in the snow. Somehow or other we got to the moment when the camera moves toward Diana, and she lifts her head, bends her bow and prepares her arrow. A difficult thing for her to do because she couldn't see and could only guess where to point the arrow. (There was no bowstring.) I think I have two good takes. Everything depends on how the eyes and the material we used for the statue turn out on the screen.

To our surprise, Doudou offered to go through the whole of this devilish scene again if the run-through isn't a success.

Her exhaustion tired me, drained me. I didn't recover my strength till about seven o'clock.

It was too much to ask her to stay in position until the take where Avenant enters the hole in the glass. I shall use a stand-in for that. I shall manage somehow. If we show just a bit of her shoulders, bow or legs, it will surely pass.

Tomorrow morning I shall do this and also Jeannot falling transfixed by the arrow.

After that we move to the terraces at the Beast's castle, which the carpenters and painters are now finishing. I'll have to use the crane for that.

We didn't know how to deal with Doudou's hair. Marais suggested that we use his Pontet wig (the one for the role of the Prince) as he's decided to dye his own hair for the part. It fitted her beautifully. We only had to plaster it with Bavox.

The set of Diana's pavilion. Avenant and Ludovic look down from the roof (p. 90).

Hammond Collection

The statue of Diana inside the pavilion (p. 92).

Tuesday the 20th, 7 a.m.

If I'm ever well enough to make a color film in Prague as Paulvé wants me to, I've found a first-class subject.

I had awful trouble with my eyes last night as the arcs had strained them. I worked out the final trick of Avenant's metamorphosis into the Beast. I won't do it yet because it requires the ruin of the two Pontet masks. The difficult thing will be to keep Marais's face in a position which must not change by a fraction of an inch, while it must continue to register terror. In successive short takes I shall film the hair invading his forehead, a cheek. I'll make one eye up, then place the fangs in position. I'll cut a long strip which I'll stick on like a stab of lightning. I shall accelerate this jigsaw until his whole face is covered. This transformation must be achieved as if it were a rain of blows, a cataclysm.

Wednesday evening, 11 o'clock.

A mixed day yesterday. At the noon run-through (the exteriors of Diana's pavilion) I saw what I wanted to see. At six I saw what I was afraid I would see—and rightly so. The inside of Diana's pavilion. The treasure doesn't shine. Diana aims badly and her eyes lose their shape as the camera approaches. These two shots ruin the joy of all the rest for me. Between the projections, I had shot, in the morning, the fall of Avenant with the Beast's face, and also his climbing through the smashed window, with Diana just in the picture. An extra stood in for Doudou. She was a beautiful, robust, simple girl.

Went to the doctor. He says I am much better in spite of still being miserably thin and tired. I had been off sugar. He says I can go back to it again. I went home, slept badly and thought of a way of doing the editing so that I can salvage my take of Diana aiming. It is more noble if one sees only her head turning and the beginning of her movement. I will cut just before the close-up. As to the treasure, I decided to have a talk with the optical effect people and have them find some way of getting these precious gems to twinkle.

Which I did as soon as I got to Saint-Maurice this morning. Then I went and had a look at the takes of Diana with Claude. Afterwards I tackled the stable set which matches up with the stuff I'd done at

Rochecorbon. The scene where the sisters rub their eyes with
onions before going up to cry to Beauty. The scene where Avenant
and Ludovic have their meeting which ends up with their riding off
on Magnificent. Sometimes in these constructed sets I think I am
in the real place and move toward a door as though it will lead me
into the manor. Then I wake up with a start.

I telescoped five shots into one. So I thought I could do the rest
(by running two shots into one). But unfortunately, Marais
stumbled over a line, and by that strange phenomenon of memory
peculiar to actors, he fluffed a dozen times on the same phrase.
This disaster was complicated by the chickens, which Clément had
to coax onto certain definite spots and there each time had to
convince them with caresses to stay still and play their part.

At last Marais got over his obstacle. But then Tiquet got his
camera all tied up in a cable and couldn't finish his pan. The simplest
thing was to break off, send the artists out for a walk, wait, relax
and have one more try after the pause. Twice Marais managed to
get over his obstacle. It was six o'clock. Alekan fixed up the lighting
for the next episode. I broke the meeting up.

I went into the auditorium, where Clément was dubbing parts
of *La Bataille du rail* that had been filmed silent. Howling in German.
The picture was projected over and over again. The cast, following
the lip movements, gave voice to the phantoms before them. The
studio dust was burning my eyes. I went home to the Palais-Royal.

Thursday evening, 10 o'clock.

This morning I did the scene where Marais opens the stable door
slightly and sticks his head out. Since he stuck his head out at
Rochecorbon, the interior was too dark and didn't match up.
I started the Rochecorbon close-up over again. We saddled Aramis
after lunch and sprinkled tinsel over his mane and tail.

I tackled the scene which presents the opposite point of view from
the one where Marais turns the horse in the courtyard and backs
into the stable. Then, the scene where he mounts. A power failure
kept us from doing the rest. This was lucky because I had just
thought of an idea that will eliminate Ludovic's trip back and forth
when he takes the bows down. The camera will come upon
Félicie taking the bows down, and she will bring them to him.
Thus she'll be in place for the mirror scene. Adélaïde will only
have to enter from the right as Ludovic mounts behind Avenant.

We will still have to film the sisters' heads and shoulders and the boys' hands and legs (as planned). Ibéria showed me the Touraine take of Aramis rearing. Unfortunately it's unusable. It's too short and badly framed. We'll have to make him rear tomorrow and with a second rider he refuses. Endless difficulties in sight. But each shot gets snatched from the void. None are easy. This profession requires courage and patience. We live in plaster and straw dust.

I found it impossible to shave this morning. The current was off from seven to eight. I took my electric razor to the studio and shaved whenever I got a chance.

Clément, who is dubbing the silent parts of *Le Rail*, is sleeping in Josette's dressing room at Saint-Maurice. I will join him there tomorrow.

The rushes of Diana's pavilion are magnificent. I can now edit the sequence except for the Avenant-Beast trick, which I won't do until last of all.

Friday the 23rd, 9 o'clock.

This morning, after the current went off at the Palais-Royal and I had to dress by candlelight, I arrived at the studio, where several power failures were to occur. Aramis was very nervous. He spent the night in his stall at Joinville. I now managed to do the mirror and bows scene as revised thanks to yesterday's power failure. Nane was very frightened of the horse. Lunch. S. and another Gaumont official came to see a run-through of several scenes. This test was important as we've gone over our estimates and Paulvé has to get Gaumont to contribute further to our costs. Everything went very well. Darbon's satisfaction showed in his great kindness. Bérard didn't like the way the great gate at the castle had been shot. Darbon offered to do it again (which is a unique gesture in the history of film producers). Bérard is rearranging the set and the shots will be done over tomorrow morning. I shot the continuation of the stable sequence. The camera, on a high boom behind the horse, takes in the boys' backs and Mila as she opens the door. I was about to film Josette on Aramis when a power failure paralyzed us. The unit dispersed. Some went to sleep in the trough in the dark stable, others wandered in the courtyard. I found Bérard with Carré. He was giving directions for the candelabras for the great hall.

In front of the door to the dressing rooms, Escoffier brought the boys one by one and dressed them with whatever he could lay his hands on. Bérard joined us and touched them up. It's incredible to see him create LeNains and Pieter de Hoochs[49] in a few minutes without a single basic costume to go on. A mysterious spectacle which professional film-makers wouldn't understand because they're used to preliminary costume designs, hired costumes, that false preciseness of the theatrical costumer. The current returned at 6:30. I went back to the set. It had lost that hallucinatory reality the blackout candles had given it and we now had to restore that truth by means of the lying lamps. Alekan got busy on it. Josette was very brave. She was frightened of Aramis because of Mila's accident in Touraine and a fall she had herself some time ago. But I had to have a shot of her on the horse and, what's more, pressing her face to its mane so that I can get away with the sleight-of-hand in the takes with her stand-in. Four times I took the picture of those two pale profiles in the moonlight: that of Aramis, his mane spangled with threads of silver, that of Josette coming in from the left and whispering the magic words: "Go where I go, Magnificent, go! go! go!" Lucile will film the stand-in tomorrow and will complete Josette's movement of straightening up on the horse as it trots off.

If Marais makes Aramis rear tomorrow, the camera will need to encounter a roof. I ordered beams, planks and straw. Michel can't be looking forward to this scene with his unhappy memories of tumbles in Touraine. (Marais assures me he isn't.) Certainly, Michel is so cheerful, charming and even-tempered that nothing makes him gloomy.

Everybody who comes here from outside and enters our film universe is amazed at our unit's harmonious relationship. They tell me that this sort of thing is rare. I wonder why. It must be torture working in the midst of rows and bad temper. The same good feelings existed among all the protagonists of L'Eternel Retour. The only thing that bothers us is that the film is progressing and the moment is approaching when we won't be living together any more. I shall miss everybody including the least workman. Not to hear the Joinville staff say "Good morning, General" in the morning chill will cause me a vexation which I don't dare contemplate.

[19][Pieter de Hooch (1629–after 1677), Dutch painter of genre scenes.]

Sunday the 24th, 9 o'clock.

A day of puttering about. Did a retake of the shots of the castle gate. But the set wasn't ready till eleven owing to yesterday's blackout. This delay threw my whole schedule out. I was supposed to finish the stable. I made the continuity girl stand in for Josette. The horse left the stable without the least spirit. I dressed Aramis's groom up as Josette and succeeded in obtaining what Corneille calls *caracoles* [capers]. The time was getting on. Alekan was nervous. I persuaded Darbon to order Aramis again for Monday morning.

In between shots (Bresson[50] and Elina had come to visit me), I ran over to the set of the great hall, where Bérard was preparing the special effect of the real human faces framed in the fireplace carvings.

In the lab this evening I saw the silent pictures of the stable. They're all right. Alekan has achieved a supernatural quality within the limits of realism. It is the reality of childhood. Fairyland without fairies. Fairyland in the kitchen.

Monday, November 26, 1945.

I have already said that it was only just that, since I covered Marais's face and hands with glue and hair, I should have suffered terrible miseries on my hands and face. This is an example of the writer's involvement which Sartre talks about. He's right. The writer who hides behind his desk is a different breed. And now the bow [*arc*] which pierces Marais at the end of the film has become for me that arc light which wounds my eyes, forehead and cheeks and which, now that my face is somewhat calmer, strikes me again in the same place. It's unbearable this evening.

This morning I shot Josette's stand-in on the horse. Then, to finish with the set, the horse rearing. To run fewer risks, I had two cameras shooting from two different angles. The horse refused three times. Out of superstition, I left the set. No sooner had I left than Marais discovered the secret language understood by a horse trained for the circus ring. He pressed with his knees and gently

---

[50] [Robert Bresson, the film director. Cocteau had written the dialogue for his film *Les Dames du Bois de Boulogne* (1945).]

pulled the bit. The horse came to a halt, thought he was being asked to back up, and, not being able to, reared. When the red light went out I returned. The shot was done.

I saw a run-through of the stuff I saw the day before yesterday, with the sound now added. Lebreton's done a wonderful job, bathing noises and voices in a gentle and strong atmosphere.

Bérard dressed (or rather disguised) the tavern companions. After lunch, I grouped them in the corner of the set, on the steps, on the ramp, behind the table. The clay pipes were lit. I distributed the Chinese cards. Alekan lit the set. Bunches of onions were hung on the walls. I told each person the business I had thought up for him. Rehearsal. Action.

The camera pans to a man smoking, an old man in a greatcoat, a little girl with her hands folded over her stomach, and comes to rest on the table where people are playing cards. All the people in the scenes know each other and not one of them looks like a walk-on. It's convincing. More convincing than reality. Truer than truth.

I finished up with the usurer's scene with Avenant and Ludovic. Closing time was drawing near. The actors fluffed their lines. We were over the time. Everybody immediately relaxed. The scene went smoothly. Even a cat wandered through as if it were at home.

Tuesday the 27th, 11 o'clock.

Terrible attack. Red streaks on my face, eyes swollen. I could hardly open them. I worked only by will power. A studio hand bought me a pair of special glasses, which eased my eyes but didn't protect them from the arcs. Tomorrow Tiquet is going to bring his, which will do this.

I shot the tavern with all the lascars whom Bérard had disguised. It's like a group by LeNain.

I've been naïve. The trick is to cut the scenes up into innumerable shots and then take several in one go. The continuity girl then puts down twelve shots and the producers are satisfied. I did the draper's final scene (the one which ends with the watch in the Beast's mirror) without a hitch.

The rushes of the continuation of the stable were fast-moving, dark, with a chiaroscuro effect, gripping. The shot of Beauty

The tavern set (p. 98).

Hammond Collection

The tavern. The draper with Avenant and Ludovic (none of the draper's scenes appears in any known print of the film).

Hammond Collection

leaning over Magnificent's neck looks like one of my drawings.

Wednesday the 28th, 8 a.m.

Very painful night. My hairy, leathery skin devoured me. My dreams became confused with my pain. The itchings became the spangles in the horse's mane. I wanted to part them. I rubbed my skin. I woke up, tortured by the swelling. I am waiting for the car. The great black hall set isn't ready. I will shoot the link-up of the Beauty–Avenant scene which we missed in Touraine and the scene of Josette doing Mila's hair.

Wednesday, 9 p.m.

Thanks to Tiquet's glasses, fitted by the studio hands with bits of black cardboard on both sides, my forehead and eyes got some rest. As the great black hall isn't ready and won't be until tomorrow (and then won't have the arms, for Bérard is having the linen that drapes them all remodeled), I had only two shots to do.

I started a retake of the Touraine shot which I didn't like of Josette–Jeannot. Now the episode links up with the scene where Beauty runs off after the sisters' dinner.

The new arc crackled. I had to take the scene seven times. We went past 12:30.

After lunch (Jourdan, Kique and Sologne[51] came to see us) I divided my time between preparing the Mila–Josette scene and the black set which Bérard is now working on. For the former it was a question of taking the glass out of Serge Roche's coral mirror, placing the camera behind it, and shooting Mila looking into the camera as though it were the mirror. After which, the camera rises to Josette, who says "I no longer dare." This mirror costs a fortune. I unscrewed it and found a sheet of wood behind. I cut this on a circular saw in the carpenter's. When we put the mirror together again, nothing will be seen. Awfully difficult shot. We hung the mirror with invisible thread. We propped it up. Finally Mila got into position behind the frame and Alekan arranged the lights. This balancing act took so long that once again I was near the time limit. I had only nine minutes left. Airplanes. Loaded the cameras again. Now I had five minutes. I was terrified of another

[51] [Madeleine Sologne, the female lead of *L'Eternel Retour*.]

blackout interrupting me. At last we were through. I asked
Lebreton and Bouboule to record Félicie's voice behind glass so
as to give the audience the impression that they are the mirror
and that they are moving up toward Beauty at the same time as
the camera.

I showed the beginning of the film to Sologne-Schlosberg,
Loulou. But it wasn't their excessive kindness, nor the praise from
the Metro-Goldwyn visitors, which gave me the most pleasure,
but one of the theater cleaners who said to Bouboule: "That's
what I call a film."

L'Eternel Retour has just won the prize at the International
Congress in Belgium.

Very fine run-through of the stable stuff, the retakes of the doors
and the beginning of the tavern scene (with the usurer and the
card game). I shall tackle the great hall set tomorrow.

Friday the 30th, 10 p.m.

I was just going to write these notes in bed when the current
went off again for the fifth time since this morning.

Yesterday blackouts and tiredness prevented me from keeping
this diary. It had been an exhausting and interesting day. Couldn't
shoot at all. It had taken too long to get under way with the black
set. We put in place and painted with Bavox the living heads
mingled with the architecture. We set up the scaffolding. We
suspended the standards. At six o'clock (Marcel André had been
made up ever since the morning but didn't complain as he's so
passionately interested in everything creative) I took two tests,
one on Kodak stock and the other on Agfa.

The lab developed them last night and we saw the results this
morning at nine. The Agfa's black is more supple and its white
more crisp. It is now clear that the set will look magnificent
provided we don't light the corners and we leave the shape of the
hall undefined, only making the sculpture stand out in relief.
(Clément, Alekan and Tiquet were pessimistic.) Having seen this
test, we made a start on this huge set, in between blackouts.
(Just as I wrote that fateful word, the lights went on again.)

I had barely written that line when they went off again. We were
working surrounded by a crowd of American visitors who,

The set of the Beast's great hall. A stone head being supplied with smoke to exhale (p. 101).

The Beast's great hall.
The Merchant at the laid
table (p. 101).

Hammond Collection

attracted by our trick shots, were perched on the flimsy steps.
The young extras who are playing the stone heads are incredibly
patient. In uncomfortable positions, kneeling behind the set, their
shoulders in a sort of armor, they must rest their hair, which is all
pomaded and Bavoxed, against the capital with the arc lamps full
in their faces. The effect is so intensely magical that I wonder if the
camera can possibly get it. These heads are alive, they *look*, they
breathe smoke from their nostrils, they turn, they follow the movements of the artists, who don't see them. Perhaps this is how the
objects which surround us behave, taking advantage of our habit
of believing them to be immobile.

I shot the Merchant's arrival (after he has passed the candelabras,
which I'll do tomorrow). The fire flames up. The clock strikes.
The table's laid, covered with plates, jugs and glasses all in the style
of Gustave Doré, on the verge of the hideous (like the Gare de Lyon).
From a confusion of pies, ivy, fruit, arises the living arm which
grasps the candlestick.

I did the close-up of the statues watching this scene. I did the
shot where the arm puts the candlestick down and picks the jug up.
I did the shot of the arm pouring (from which I will cut to a shot
of Marcel looking terrified). Time was up. We dispersed. Darbon
is worried that the film isn't going to be long enough. I'll take
advantage of this and make it longer, by emphasizing details
which will create an uneasy atmosphere. Aldo and the reporters
wanted me to take my glasses off so that they could photograph
me beside the living statues. The arcs seized the opportunity and
stabbed me. The red bags formed under my eyes immediately.

After numerous takes of the stone heads, I used my usual method.
I ran away, leaving Clément to carry on alone. He and his wife
Bella are wonderful people. My work has become theirs. While
Clément was directing the head movements, Ibéria took me off
to choose the first shots of Diana's pavilion.

At seven we were shown the end of the tavern. Thanks to Alekan,
Tiquet, Bérard, Michel, Marais (who's absolutely first-rate in the
scene near the table) and to everyone else in it, this sequence has
turned out enchanting.

Roger Hubert has received a fat bonus from Paulvé for our
award in Belgium. Sologne and Marais may possibly go to
Brussels tomorrow morning.

Saturday evening, December 1, 1945.

However much I may shut myself up in my own unreal and private world, it's impossible for me not to be interested in the Nuremberg trial. Goering's mad laugh as he slaps his thighs, and suddenly everything is dark except for the heads of the accused picked out with ghostly spots. The film of the German atrocities is shown. Those who allowed or ordered these horrors from afar see it all and lose their composure. Goering's face becomes like that of a very old, sick woman.

Worked with Bérard on the black set from 9 a.m. till 6:30 p.m. without a break. I'm allowing myself the luxury of lingering over details, for I've noticed from the rushes that the film moves along at top speed, like *Les Enfants Terribles* and *Thomas l'Imposteur*.[52] I must make the sequence in the Beast's castle more relaxed and quiet, a different tempo.

I found that Alekan's lighting on the living statue heads was too bright and made them look too human. I started to do it again, having first plastered their heads with dark paint as if the fire had licked them. Immediately their eyes shone and the heads blended in with the mouldings. A magnifying glass on a test shot proves it's now all right.

Tiquet said it would be a mistake not to have a shot of the arms holding the candlesticks when Marcel André gets up from the table. He was right. I gave the necessary orders. But the candelabras, hanging from invisible threads, swung at the ends of the isolated arms. Carré thought of black supports. The studio hands built them. After an hour's work, the supports were invisible against the walls, and the candelabras stood up straight. This forest of lights looked strange. Clément added the liveliness of taper flames thanks to the waving of a piece of plywood. I got that shot which had seemed impossible to film before next week. At 6:15 I did a shot which I had thought of when I noticed the lion's head at the end of the chair arm. The Merchant's hand *is sleeping* on this lion's head. When the Beast's roar is heard in the distance, the hand *wakes up* and escapes. On Monday I'll do a shot of the candle stumps in the candelabras, from which I'll cut to Marcel's fear and

---

[52] [Here, of course, Cocteau is referring to his novels, since the film versions postdated the present diary. *Thomas l'Imposteur* was first published in 1923; Georges Franju's film version appeared in 1965, after Cocteau's death. *Les Enfants Terribles* was first published in 1929; Jean-Pierre Melville's film version (made with Cocteau's participation) appeared in 1950.]

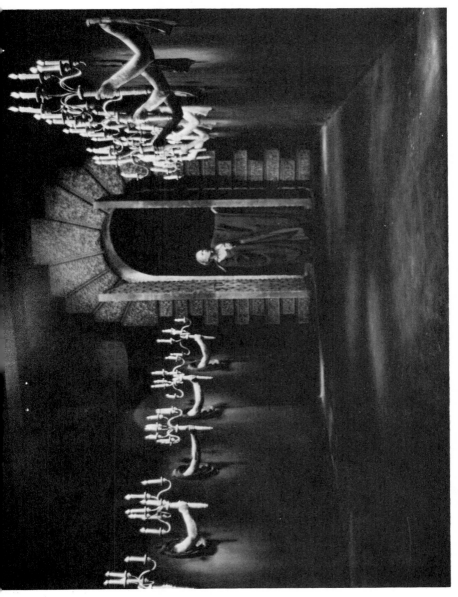

The Beast's great hall.
Beauty enters under the
candelabras (p. 104).

Hammond Collection

The Beast's great hall. The Beast carries Beauty, who has fainted at her first sight of him, to her room.

Hammond Collection

the beginning of his flight.

The arcs have burnt my eyelids and cheeks again. Burns on top of burns. I'm paying dearly for this film.

Monday—Tuesday, 3 o'clock.

Two frantic days at full pressure wondering whether anyone else would get this worked up over a film. But I believe I'm right, for I am producing images that contain violence, heat, a pulsation of strength, dust and light. That is a consolation for the interminable waiting, the candles that refuse to go out even under the tempest of the wind machine, the inopportune unionism of the extras. This evening (we'd been over and over the same scene since morning) we were just at the point of getting the right rhythm, the human arms holding the candlesticks were going to bend and unbend properly, when the arms left their posts with the excuse that this last take would run overtime by one minute.

The run-through consoled me. It was both rich and sensitive. Lady Diana and Miss Churchill came and lunched with us. I showed them the first scenes of the film. They were disappointed that they couldn't see it all. (I can see nothing any more but my own mistakes.)

Nuremberg trial. The two-and-two-make-four's are judging the two-and-two-make-five's or even twenty-two.

I almost loathe setting down the details of these sickening retakes, with all the paraphernalia of motors, the lamps that must be turned on and off in accord with the wind blowing out the candles (which, since I am filming this episode in reverse, will appear to be illuminated one by one). If I put them down it is because I cannot praise highly enough the patience, courage and skill of Alekan, Tiquet, Clément, this matchless unit. To hold the slightest threads of this enormous and delicate mechanism, which I survey from the top of the black stairs; to subdue so much dust, independent wills, ingenious disorder; to call for action, interrupt it (because a thread breaks), resume and never lose hold of the big picture—this is an example of that sublime integrity which is disappearing from France.

My face is very red and swollen this evening. My forehead sweats and looks as if it's been varnished. Grémillon[53] told Jeannot

---

[53][Presumably Jean Grémillon (1902–1959), French film director whose admirable career began in silent days; he was President of the Cinémathèque Française from 1943 to 1958.]

at Brussels that he'd had the same trouble for three months but it mysteriously disappeared overnight.

Wednesday evening.

Another day snatched from pain, from that huge black room from which we emerge like chimney sweeps. Charles Trénet,[54] the Marquise, Rosine and her son lunched with us. This morning I did the slow-motion shot of Josette coming into the hall under the candelabras. From after lunch until evening, the slow motion of her going up the grand staircase. We mounted the camera on the big crane and followed her up.

We exhausted ourselves, losing time in last-minute details and finishing touches. The dust which her rapid movement (necessitated by the slow motion) raises may look very noble and rich on the screen. At the head of the stairs one of the caryatids turns its head to the right, the armored arms lift the curtain, Josette enters the corridor. All of this very fast (eighty-frame slow motion). To-morrow I will tackle the scenes of Beauty and the Beast round the table. I'll do the ensembles before the set's broken up. A run-through (backwards) of the candles lighting of their own accord. It looks exactly as though it had been taken straight. The style recalls Méliès, Robert Houdin,[55] *Le Sang d'un Poète.* Plenty of harshness, somewhat fierce surprise, violence. I like this style and prefer it to what I expected.

Last night I thought up a new sequence which I'll put in before the scene where Beauty sees the Beast drinking. I needed a slow, silent scene in which Beauty is torn between terror and her rustic courage. I will place it near the caryatid at the top of the stairs, in the corridor, behind the bust and in Beauty's room. The Beast offers her the pearl necklace which she wears at Epinay and which she will pretend not to wear in the hunting-dog terrace scene.

---

[54][Outstanding French popular songwriter and singer, born 1913; Cocteau helped him to achieve his great success in the Thirties.]

[55][Georges Méliès (1861–1938) was the great French pioneer of imaginative movie-making, who started producing his brief fantasy films before the turn of the century. Robert Houdin (1805–1871) was the greatest French professional magician of the nineteenth century. When Méliès' film career began, he was the owner of the theater Houdin had built.]

The lighting of the
Beast's great hall set.

Hammond Collection

The corridor set. Beauty
sees the Beast walking at
night (p. 106).

Hammond Collection

Thursday evening.

Things went well. Did the whole of Beauty's first dinner in the great hall. Finished shots round the table and in front of the fireplace with one of the living statues, by a swoop of the small crane, and the departure of the Beast behind Josette's chair. He goes through the arch, turns around one last time and closes the iron gate. We see him disappearing behind it.

Bérard was there. He did Josette's headdress (jet sequins and ostrich feathers) and arranged Jeannot's cloak. Now that Jeannot was made up as the Beast again, he was back in the same old mood and refused to lunch. We insisted and brought him a little minced meat and mashed potatoes.

Had a look at the corridor with Bérard, marked out where to put the statues, corrected mistakes in Beauty's room. Jeannot suggests that we play *Les Parents Terribles* in Brussels instead of *Renaud et Armide,* which takes so long to prepare. He phoned de Bray and Dorziat.[56] There's some difficulty over dates.

My skin is drying, swelling, getting rough, getting smooth. The boils are doing their best to return. Endless struggle.

Saturday, December 8, 1945.

Yesterday, Friday, did the second table scene. Kept very close to my first shooting script. I did the whole scene in two takes. I'll put the close-ups in this morning. Josette was so tired on Thursday, Alekan was afraid that it would show. The rushes betray a suspicious diffuseness. I was told about "intermediate focus" and other excuses. In the car, Josette confessed to me that she was frightened of being photographed too sharp.

Her face looked rested yesterday so I asked Alekan to return to the style I like. I added a peacock with its feathers to the table. Josette paces up and down in front of the fireplace, her movement followed by the left-hand caryatid's eyes. The camera tilts up to the clock, then to the mirror in which you see the Beast's reflection as he comes down the staircase at the back.

---

[56] [*Renaud et Armide:* play by Cocteau, 1943. Yvonne de Bray and Gabrielle Dorziat: actresses long associated with Cocteau.]

Monday morning, 7 o'clock.

Shot by shot I must win the match. That is, I must never leave Saint-Maurice ill at ease; I must fulfil my creative wishes completely. I decided yesterday, Sunday, that Marais should play *Les Parents Terribles* in Brussels and that Reggiani[57] should continue in Paris while Marais produced *Renaud et Armide* in Belgium and Switzerland. Madame Rolle, director of the Théâtre du Gymnase, phoned to say that Reggiani has signed up for three films and won't be free. Which means a great financial loss for Marais and me, for I don't expect there'll be any other free dates. Feuillère[58] would like to create *Azraël* in October, after *Les Parents.*

We can work today, tomorrow, and the day after from 7:30 to 5:30 as the electricity cuts have been restored. After which we shall no doubt work at night, which I prefer. Cold (twenty-two degrees of frost). Which is worrying as Josette has to wear the Paquin *déshabillé.* Bérard's coming at midday to do her hair and finish the corridor set.

Tuesday the 11th, 9 p.m.

Two days of chaos, because I was changing sets and going from one set to another creates such havoc with moving all the gear that it looks like a cataclysm. The ruins of an abandoned set are those of a childhood home. Memories of the old set overwhelm us when we're in the new one, and so on. It'll surely be a sinister day when the film ends.

Today I started the sequence I thought up on the night of December 5th. Bérard has put two very beautiful busts in the corridor. They are two Louis XIV Turks in marble. I shall make Beauty hide behind one of these when she sees the Beast walking in the corridor at night as though in a trance. His hands are smoking and she looks at them for the first time with horror. The Beast has just made a kill.

The moonlight and candlelight were supernatural, but unfortunately the run-through shows that our Agfa stock must be stale and needs excess light. We must resign ourselves to losing

[57][Serge Reggiani (born 1922), noted stage and film actor.]

[58] [The great stage and film actress Edwige Feuillère (born 1907). *Azraël* was the working title of Cocteau's play *L'Aigle à Deux Têtes;* Feuillère and Marais created the leading roles in 1946. Cocteau's film version with the same two stars appeared in 1947 (Bérard was art director of both the play and the film).]

details and seeing something different from what we saw, something still beautiful but more subdued.

It took half a day to get Marais's hands ready. It is like the ritual the Chinese actors go through.

I shall go on with the corridor tomorrow. (Beauty's arrival as she comes up the corridor without moving her feet, thanks to a string-pulling arrangement, and the memorable scene of which the first rushes made Paulvé decide to finance us.)

It was Marais's birthday. Carpenters, electricians and dressers brought him a basket of roses with a card: "To our good Beast."

December 13th, 1945, 6 p.m.

We're not yet as bad as those princes of Java who rehearse a dance for five years, but we've been five hours making up Marais's head and hands.

I am writing this in the make-up room. It's six o'clock. We are shooting at nine. In line with my permanent unconventionality, shooting at night doesn't upset my life much, except that I'm living at the Hôtel du Louvre so my sleep won't be interrupted by phone calls and visitors as it would be at the Palais-Royal. Breakfast at seven o'clock in the evening and the same rhythm for the rest of the night. I was supposed to come at 8:30 this evening. I came with Marais because I wanted to see if Carré had broken down the statues which stand at the top of the stairs. For you can hardly pick them out on the screen. I will place them in the corners of Beauty's room and make use of them there. This room is now taking shape. Its net walls, its décor of rocks à la Mantegna[59] which can be made out through them, the brambles that invade the room, the bed shaped like a boat and with a ram's head, the window, the stone door, the grass on the floor—all this gives me excellent opportunities.

I must finish the corridor tonight. The magic mirror scene; the one where the Beast carries Beauty in his arms into her room; the Beast seen from Beauty's point of view in the scene "What are you doing outside my room at such an hour?"

While I write this on the marble-topped make-up table, at my right Marais and Arakelian start on the head and tear the shirt with

[59][The Italian painter and engraver Andrea Mantegna (1431–1506) used craggy rocks in many of his compositions.]

the enormous shoulders (Marais's head make-up throws his normal shoulders off balance). I intend to abandon the Agfa stock when we do Beauty's room. As it loses detail and adds blackness, it was excellent for the oppressive atmosphere of the hall scene. But Beauty's room in the castle must be light as air, representing an effort of the Beast in the direction of graciousness.

Night filming reminds me of Christmas as a child when I was allowed to stay up late, and of the vigil for the presents and the deep snow around the house with its myriad lights. Unfortunately the unit find it merely exhausting and a nuisance.

I like this factory at Saint-Maurice, as I liked the nursing home at Saint-Cloud when I wrote *Opium* and *Les Enfants Terribles* there. Green[60] brought me the proofs of *Leviathan*. I explored the old conservatory of the Pozzo di Borgo balls in the moonlight. I saw Elizabeth weaving her linen there.

This evening, alone at Saint-Maurice, I wander through the corridors, the sound stages, the parts of sets being built or demolished. My dream possesses me. This snow of childhood Christmases, this light, phosphorescent snow carries me away. It is a white tablecloth spread in my heart.

Saturday, December 15th.

I've never seen a set either in the theater or in films that appealed as much to me as this one of Beauty's room where I'm working now. It casts a spell. The studio hands like it. The waitresses from the restaurant come and see it and are ecstatic.

I'd like to hear this room described by Poe; it is built in the air, in space, in the midst of the remnants of my forest and the beginnings of my future spring set. With the result that through its walls of net, invaded by thorn bushes, a whole incomprehensible landscape can be made out. Its carpet is of grass and its furniture in the magnificent bad taste of Gustave Doré. I have placed the living statues amidst bushes in the corners on either side of the door. Behind the transparent wall I have hung the candelabra, which are held by plastered arms outside. It looks magnificent in the pale beams of the arc even though they do hurt my eyes.

We've worked from nine o'clock in the evening to six in the

---

[60] [The novelist Julien Green, born in America in 1900, most of whose books have been in French. *Leviathan* was first published in 1929.]

The Beast as seen by Beauty when she asks: "What are you doing outside my room at such an hour?" (p. 107).

Hammond Collection

Beauty's bed in the Beast's castle, with its decoration of vines (p. 109). The Beast watching Beauty after she has fainted.

Hammond Collection

morning. I was at the studio at seven. I myself decorated the bed with vines, arranged the furniture and fitted out the dressing table. It takes such a time getting a set like this ready. It was three in the morning before I was able to do the panning shot round the room which is illuminated in sectors* and the first scene of Josette's entrance (when the mirror speaks to her). Between two takes I went to see a run-through of the moving floor in the corridor and the close-up of Marais to be spliced into the scene where he looks at his hands. They're all right. You wonder how Josette glides along the ground without moving her feet.

I slept at the Hôtel du Louvre. They were moving furniture out on the floor above, so I didn't sleep very well. I went to the Palais-Royal for breakfast at five and am now writing these notes in the make-up room at Saint-Maurice.

Flu, eczema, arc burns. How will I hold out? There are still three weeks to go.

Sunday.

I worked till seven in the morning. Came home at eight. In bed by nine. Awakened by Julien Green and his sister Anne, who took me out to lunch. I got back to bed at four. Shall go to the studio tomorrow at seven. Day work. This alternation upsets everything. Marais kept his make-up on for fifteen hours. I no longer dared ask him to do a retake. Some night visitors came and had a look at us working in Beauty's set, but they soon got tired. They couldn't believe that film work demanded such efforts. They watched. They got exhausted. They left. And the martyrdom of the arcs, of the alternating heat and cold, went on. But this *had* to be attempted once: a poet telling a story through the medium of the camera. I know people blame me for exhausting myself over a film. They are wrong.

Tuesday the 18th, 7:30 a.m.

Awful night. This inflammation which invades my body and devours my armpits causes me great suffering. At Saint-Maurice the work often takes my mind off it. It's at home that pain triumphs. For two days I've been struggling with all sorts of difficulties in

* Later I cut out this take.

Beauty's room. I'm wondering how things are turning out and am anxious for a run-through. But the lab is behind. When they do develop any rushes, they're out of order and not the ones I really need to see. The Agfa is harsh and doesn't seem to be able to get the sparkling transparency of this ethereal room. I used Diot, the apprentice assistant, for the Beast yesterday. He could easily pass for Marais. The mask gave him the same sad animal look and elicited the same gestures (putting his hands up to his mouth and eyes to fasten the mask). I did a shot of him moving behind the veils, on the corridor side, before the scene. "What are you doing in my room?"* Beauty, doing her hair, feels a presence there. She takes the candlestick from the living hand and moves toward the door. Then I took the shots of Josette representing Jeannot's point of view as he stands outside her door. I have seen these takes on the screen. It's quite magnificent, but the memory of the try-out bothers me. This morning I must retake a close-up of the Beast roaring. The half-length image is not forceful enough. I have yet to do Josette going out backwards and I will begin the scenes of Jeannot in her room (when he comes in after she has disappeared by magic, approaches her empty bed and sniffs the fur coverlet).

Fatigue, illness and the alternation of night and day work confuse me and keep me from seeing the film as a whole, though I am aware of the violent beauty of the isolated shots.

I must become more serene—more like a flowing river. I'll try to take myself in hand.

It's impossible to answer the letters that are piling up. Impossible to answer my friends' calls. Paul has bought me a car. He's looking for a chauffeur. I have just been out in this car to get a breath of fresh air somewhere or other, to escape from this filth that envelops us and impregnates us.

There's nothing more terrible than a film which is shot from beginning to end without a break. You wonder if you won't collapse before the finish.

Thursday, December 20, 1945.

I haven't kept these notes regularly because the end of a film like ours bears the accelerated weight of all that has gone before and demands an enormous effort to keep in balance. I have tried to get

---

* I had cut out this passage. On the screen he no longer resembled him.

In Beauty's room (the scene of the gift of the necklace). The Beast,
who has just made a kill, looks at his smoking fingers.

Beauty's bedroom in
the Beast's castle. She
is wearing the magic
glove that transports
her between the castle
and her home.

the maximum intensity into even incidental shots. The studios are hired and waiting. Our successors are threatening the firm. Joinville says that I am going over the electricity quota. In short, I have to struggle with difficulties that shouldn't enter my calculations. In Beauty's room yesterday I skipped over several of these problems. I will skip over some tonight; Darbon has asked me to finish the scene of the golden key (balcony of the room on the brink of the void) between 9 p.m. and 8 a.m. I have done Beauty's disappearances and reappearances.

I had thought of dubbing the voice of the Beast, changing Marais's voice, having it imitated by a deep voice. Experience shows me it's impossible. The vocal characterization he brings to the part can't be imitated. As soon as one uses a double for him— even a skilled one—the spell is broken. Jacques Lebreton is preparing a filter which will modify Marais's own voice.

When we have finished shooting (in about two weeks) I will begin the film, as it were. I will have to do the editing and mixing and find the places for Georges's[61] music. I will have to impress upon him his rhythm and mine.

Yesterday in the courtyard at Saint-Maurice I saw the winged horse which Bérard wants to add to the spring set. On Monday afternoon I shall shoot the two sets (one scene each) which finish Marcel André's part.

December 22, 1945.

The torture continues. I have an abscess forming under a neglected tooth which is driving me mad. I got back from work at eight o'clock this morning. I got to bed at nine and at ten woke up in such a state that I had to throw on some clothes and rush to the dentist. I suffered so much from my inflammation and my toothache on the night before last that I couldn't control myself any more, went all to pieces and was unable to direct properly. The living statues were fainting in their plaster shells. They were carried into the air. They came to, insisted on being made up again, and fainted a second time. I got back to the Hôtel du Louvre in the morning only to find I'd been shifted to a miserable room next to a telephone booth where people shout all the time. Couldn't sleep

---

[61] [Georges Auric (born 1899) wrote music for many Cocteau plays and films. He was one of the composers in the post-World War I "Groupe des Six," all friends of Cocteau.]

a wink. But thanks to this insomnia, I thought of a way of combining several shots and giving a splendid finish to the sequence. Yesterday I got rid of all the work we'd done the day before and shot this new stuff. Marais was excellent. The run-through had some beautiful work in it.

This afternoon, visited the sets for the end with Bérard, who gave his instructions.

It's raining. I'm freezing. I'm miserable. On Monday I'll shoot the port official's house and harbor scene.

Christmas Day, 1945.

There's never been a proper Christmas since I was a child. We never get that deep warm snow any more and I loathe the parody of it. I never have a festive Christmas meal. I dined at B.'s last night, then came home to bed. I had worked the whole day in the legal office and the harbor. I finished with Marcel at five o'clock. In the office I dressed Carrier as the bailiff's clerk and turned the stage carpenters into fishermen, which, of course, the unions don't allow. But they were good enough to waive the matter and the union officials themselves turned a blind eye to it. Thus I had simple, real characters who did not add an alien style to the film. Bérard and Escoffier made costumes for them out of nothing but a few rags. The camera, perched on the small crane, turned the corner of the house, caught Marcel's exit and the slamming door, and on the square (in the added panel) came across the bailiff going out of the other door of the office. Marcel passes him on his horse. The bailiff cries ironically: "Bon voyage." The horse goes on up the street at the end of which we can see the parapet, the boats, the houses by the shore, and then it turns off to the right behind the column of a fish market. A child with a crutch crosses the empty street. The fishermen, seated on the ground, are repairing a large brown net near a woman who sits by her stall heaped with oysters and fish (Volpère had brought a car full).—Everything was most relaxed, running as smoothly as a watch.

A run-through at 5:30 to see the stuff which I took the night when I was making a mess of everything, when the living statues were fainting and I had to plaster an apprentice in their place—when Tiquet and Alekan told me that the best thing was to scrap the whole night's work. The scene is excellent. The statue is perfect.

The harbor set (p. 112).

Hammond Collection

The spring set (p. 113). During one of their strolls, the Beast drinks from Beauty's hands.

Hammond Collection

So I shall keep this stuff up my sleeve in case the retakes we did aren't what I like to see. I constantly regretted having to cut out bits of intense poetry. But one mustn't, at any cost, be seduced by an attractive idea if it hasn't got its right place.

Whatever happens I will keep the shot of the living statue and will put it in after the pan shot round Beauty's room. It is the final corner of the room and looks toward the door where Beauty is standing. Her glance moves to the left and furnishes the take-off point for the pan shot.

After the run-through, Bérard and I climbed over the ruins of the room to get the spring ready. It's my last set. I feel most depressed. All this exhausting work evaporates and leaves us nothing but its reflection. These places where we have labored, struggled and suffered together become new places inhabited by tenants who treat us like visiting strangers.

Here is the spring, the dirty water, the rocks, the grotto, the dripping wall, the winged horse that will look at the swans. Here is the place where I will once more get worked up, suffer and forget my suffering.

Tuesday, 11 p.m., December 25th.

I have just come back from dining at the British Embassy, where we had a Christmas tree. Georges Auric was at my table and we talked about the music he's to write. He'll start next week.

The amazing advance public attention to this film is surely due not so much to us (I mean to the curiosity our undertaking arouses) as to that Beauty and Beast we thrilled over as children. Happily, there is some remnant of childhood in this jaded public. It is this childhood we must reach. It is the incredulous reserve of the adults that we must overcome.

Friday, December 28, 1945, 8:30 p.m., Saint-Maurice.

What with the torments I am undergoing, and having to work at night and sleep in the daytime at the Hôtel du Louvre, I haven't been able to keep these notes for a few days. Between the Beast and Prince Charming, I will film trick shots. I will do the very last bit on Wednesday. Out of prudence I'll cut up the Beast's mask tomorrow. In case I can't do it this way, Alekan tried last night to see if it could be done simply by reflection. Otherwise it will take three hours, and during that time, Marais mustn't move a fraction of an inch. Last night I shot the scenes where the Beast is dying. I had put collars on the swans' necks. They managed to tear them off in an hour. Their angry struggles made them look like the arabesques of a monogram. Chance provided me with genuine stylistic discoveries which would create insoluble problems if premeditated. The swans were furious at this unknown animal whose mane and paw hung limp in the water. They attacked it and hissed. Marais, with his usual calm, didn't flinch, but let them come on. These swans attacking their sick master, deprived of his power, added great strangeness to the scene. I like this last set. The winged horse is reflected in the spring's flowing water. The moon illumines a pool of ink.

The day before, lapping this water, Marais invented a striking pantomine for the Beast drinking. He drank some water, tossed his head and spat out again. He actually *drank* this disgusting water. No other artist I know would have done that.

Sunday the 29th, 8 p.m.

I woke at six at the Hôtel du Louvre. Breakfast at seven at the Palais-Royal. The car's coming to fetch me at 8:30.

From eight yesterday to eight this morning, I left things clear for Alekan and Tiquet to do their trick transformation of Avenant into the Beast. Marais as Avenant and Diot as the Beast had to stay motionless, one on each side of a glass, and superimpose their images one on another, as those of Pasteur were in the Berville[62] shop window of my childhood.

Besides that, I shot the model of Diana's pavilion and the magic mirror held in Beauty's hands. I have seen a run-through of the bailiff and harbor. Excellent. I have chosen the corridor takes.

The rest of the time, I suffered as usual from my germs, amidst the hubbub of a trick shot session. Tonight I shall try my way of doing it. Marais will have to remain completely immobile for three hours while he's made up bit by bit. If he moves a hundredth of an inch he'll ruin a take. That's why I've left Alekan to get on with it. If my idea doesn't work . . . I'll fall back on one of his.

[62] [Berville-sur-Mer, on the Normandy coast.]

I shall try and finish with Josette (retake of her listening to Marais) and the shot where the pearl necklace forms by magic on the Beast's hand (which will project backwards in slow motion).

On Wednesday, after the Christmas holiday, I'll make a start on Prince Charming using Rochester stock, which is softer and more precise than Agfa and Kodak.

Clément hopes to shoot the fake clouds in the courtyard at Saint-Maurice if it doesn't rain.

Sunday, 9 a.m.

I have just returned from Saint-Maurice. I loathe factory work. I like improvisation and modest resources which stimulate my imagination. But there are limits. I spent the night fighting a slow-motion camera, a sort of antique sewing machine which has to be slung upside down for filming backwards, which goes askew and scratches the film. The big wall trick was remarkable except for the preparation of the hole; the paper stuck too quickly and then, being too short, showed the shape of the door behind it. As a result it was just a night of tests. I shall have to do this sleight-of-hand stunt and the pearls forming one by one on the Beast's hand all over again, as the film got scratched. I did Josette's link-up shot.

The big crane worked very well in giving the illusion of a trap door. Josette slowly and gently disappears into the wall.

But what hitches we've had were made up for by the run-through of the spring sequence, which is really splendid. I even think I'll keep Alekan's way of changing Avenant into the Beast. There is one version where the fangs grow, the face blurs and the eyes are covered with shadows and hair, which will be absolutely first-class for editing. It would spare me the terrible work which my way would have entailed. I am in a hurry to finish the spring on Wednesday or Thursday and have the bulk of the film in hand. I will have nothing left but trick shots with back projections.

Out in the courtyard, while I was struggling with planks and cables, Clément was taking his clouds, which he made with German smoke. If the negative's scratched, they'll have to do it all over again.

Monday.

Here we are at the very last day of 1945. Whatever happens to us in France, we ought to remind ourselves constantly that we are in France and that the worst intestine squabbles are preferable to an occupation. I am an expert on occupation. I'm being occupied by germs. The new inflammation from which I now suffer reminds me of the grey canker which has only just disappeared. How grateful I'd be if anybody could liberate me from my germs. Praise be to those who cured France of hers. The rest is nothing but discomfort.

I have made notes on the rhythm for the credits. All I have yet to do is to set up the false clapper board and the names and take shots of Bérard and Auric. I am trying to find material for the flying cloak. Misia says there is a kind of plant satin which hangs with many fine folds.

If Sert[63] were living, he'd have opened his Ali Baba coffers for me and I'd have drawn forth splendors. But Sert is dead and his door's sealed up.

Wednesday, 11 p.m.

First days of 1946. Eaten alive, I woke up feeling worse and worse and determined to finish my work.

I have only one day and one night left at the studio to do scenes which require ten. I know how these schedules work out. On paper they mean something, in practice nothing. A thousand unforeseen difficulties arise. The end of a film creates a sort of fever of clumsiness. Everybody falls over everybody else. Eight-thirty in the morning becomes eleven o'clock. The artists have to be made up one at a time; their hair has to be set; then they put on their new costumes and find they need breaking in. Trick shots which seem so simple once you've decided how you're going to do them raise insurmountable technical problems when you're ready for them. I will try the impossible but it seems to me we shall have to obtain one day's grace (at least) at the studios or else take ourselves elsewhere. Marais looks supremely elegant as Prince Charming. He made a sensation when he went into the canteen, which was full of the *Collier de la Reine* crowd. I have done the first scenes of the

---

[63] [José Maria Sert (1876–1945), Spanish painter and set and costume designer active in Paris. Misia (Edwards) Sert was his talented wife.]

The spring set. Beauty returns to save the dying Beast.

Hammond Collection

Prince Charming (Jean Marais) by the spring (p. 117).

episode where Beauty finds her Beast changed into Prince Charming. I have left the trick shot where he stands up (shot backwards) for tomorrow.

Thursday the 3rd, 7:30.

In my little red room at the Palais-Royal, I am looking at the Gustave Doré piece which I've just had cast in bronze. It's this object which is at the bottom of this film. It summarizes and explains it. It's incredible how much a work of art can influence you subconsciously. This group of Perseus, Andromeda and the dragon wouldn't be out of place in Beauty's room at the Beast's castle.

Holding a steel lance which prises the monster's jaws, Perseus, mounted on Bellerophon, almost erect in his stirrups between the wings of the horse, swings above the mélange of woman and volutes of scales. The base, in the style of 1900, is like a furious wave. Each time I walk up and down the room, the steel lance vibrates and the horse and hero quiver. I want to end the film in this style and find a way of using the clouds which we filmed in the courtyard that will be equally unusual.

Perhaps Clément and I will use a glass and combine the reflection of the clouds with that of the flying pair.

Friday, January 4, 1946, 7 p.m.

We are going to work at night. The last night. I know of nothing so sad as the end of a film and a unit that has worked well together breaking up. Even a studio hand feels this little death. The work that I've got left is difficult. The Prince and Beauty start to fly. The Prince and Beauty fly through the clouds. Beauty comes through the wall into her father's room. Tricks, but straightforward ones, the only kind I like, invent and insist on getting right.

Yesterday I finished the takes of Prince Charming by the spring. Marais was a prince and he was charming. I ended up with a shot of him falling backwards, in reverse and slow motion, so that he will appear to rise in a single bound with an otherworldly grace. But in spite of the work they're doing and the help they're giving, Alekan, Tiquet and Clément are beginning to live elsewhere.

Clément has to scout out the exteriors for the Noël–Noël[64] film. Alekan is to prepare a film with Stroheim, with Tiquet as assistant.[65] We are no longer all held within the same dream. Each of us is beginning to wake up.

Even if I finish my schedule by tomorrow morning, I will still have the back projections to do. The rooms for this work aren't free. We will have to wait, then some Sunday get the scattered organism of *Beauty and the Beast* together, edit my film, knowing that the finishing touches are missing, and remain suspended in space.

I will start the editing next week. That is the true rhythm of my work. *My handwriting.* Anyone else would hand back my manuscript page *corrected*, recopied in round hand or running hand.

Ibéria, who intuits what I want, tries to do me that impossible favor: writing my handwriting. But her work eases my task so that I don't get lost in a hopeless coil of film. She also lends calmness, grace and discretion.

My germs tortured me less yesterday but now they're worse again. After I've finished the studio work, I'll go and see the doctor again. I have done exactly what he told me to do.

Saturday, January 5, 1946, 8 o'clock, Saint-Maurice.

Naturally I came back to Joinville. Last night it was evident we were at the end. We were in a hurry, and so we just marked time. Many visitors. The young woman standing in for Josette was too tall and clumsy. I said to myself: "She is going to sprain her ankle right at the start." She twisted her toes at the third jump and fell, dragging Jeannot down with her. I will have all the takes printed and try to use the stuff we've taken in slow motion after the fall.

In order to get material to use, I did a shot of Marais arriving with Josette in his arms. He puts her down. We take a shot of them down to the waist as they come toward the camera. They dive in and out in such a way that I will begin the reverse movement with the shot going in the normal direction. But there will be very little left to use.

The back projections and the glass shots, the shots of clouds and

[64][Popular French comedian, singer and songwriter (born 1897; real name Lucien Noël) who appeared in numerous films. His film directed by Clément was *Le Père Tranquille* (1946).]
[65][Stroheim made two French films in 1946: *La Foire aux Chimères*, directed by Pierre Chenal, and *On ne meurt pas comme ça!*, directed by Jean Boyer.]

the earth receding, raise problems which can't be solved immediately. I shall edit a film without an ending, waiting for an end to come.

Darbon has given us one more night. That's why we are in the make-up room at Saint-Maurice this evening. I will do the shot of Josette between the wall she passes through (done last night) and the shot at the base of the wall where she moves forward toward Marcel André. I will film the couple on the platform of the big crane with the small crane going in reverse. If I can get the actors moved till they block the lens, I will be free to unblock it from the opposite point of view and place them either in the clouds or against the background of the receding earth.

At any rate, I don't like the uncertainty about the ending. I would have liked to have my hand on all the visual material.

Sunday, 4:30 a.m.

We have just finished the night session. Shot of the shadow of the glove on Beauty's face. Shot using both cranes. Beauty and the Prince flying against the background of a bird's-eye view of the spring set.

Duverger has had a magnificent moviola put in the cutting room for me. I can start work quickly, without the worries I had about the old moviola. A moviola is the machine that allows us to see and hear the film on a reduced scale, to stop it at any point and turn it backward or forward.

I will take the shots of Bérard, Auric and myself on Tuesday (for the credits). On Monday I will arrange with Orin when to do the back projections.

Sunday, 5 p.m.

I have just woken up after a medley of absurd and, as always, entirely *coherent* dreams. They constitute another life which I have to live even in the most trivial details.

The end of the film, which saddened me at Joinville, doesn't sadden me this morning, which is an evening. The instinct I have for writing an act of a play to a proper length without timing it has enabled me to accomplish the work of the last two nights outside the limit of the job, after the goal. The reel has been completed in my soul.

All that's left of that terrible toy factory which excites us and absorbs our nervous strength is a single magical toy: the moviola, which reminds me of the miniature theater of *Monsieur le Vent et Madame la Pluie*.[66] In a piece of rough glass no bigger than a cigarette case I shall see my sets and characters live again. I will interrupt them and start them off again whenever I like. I will force them to go backward or forward in time as I wish.

Praise to the Parisian worker. The matériel doesn't hold up any more—their genius replaces it. I use the word genius in the Stendhalian familiar sense.

I'm always asking studio hands to do the impossible. They never answer: "It's impossible." They look for things. They find things. Excuse me. They find things. They look for things. The search follows the discovery. They find first.

You can set them any problem. They answer: "That can be done." They disappear. They come back with nails, planks, supports. They meditate. They discuss the job. They build. They're so interested in their work that they are oblivious of the sound unit's efforts to keep them quiet. No sooner has the last word been recorded than the hammers and saws are at it again. I wonder how seriously they take the work of the actors. In the bus to Joinville a big woman was talking about *Le Collier de la Reine*. Somebody asked her if she was an actress. "Oh, no!" she replied, "I work. I'm an assistant make-up girl."

A bivouac has sprung up around the charcoal brazier. Stars and technicians warm up together. They describe their campaigns. That is, their last films.

Friday, January 11, 1946.

I have finished. In other words, I'm beginning. I have harvested my images. It only remains for me to merge them with one another and give them a movement which will have to be very subtle, since this tale contains no salient point and unfolds to a slow rhythm without real drama. You can't hope to arouse emotion or elicit tears. You must please at all costs, or displease. Period.

Last Monday I was filming in the photography studio, where we've been relegated by the new productions. I did some close-ups

[66] [Play by Paul de Musset (1804-1880); perhaps Cocteau is referring to some film version.]

which I'll insert in the final Prince Charming scene and some trick takes shot against black velvet. My final link-up shots, in a month, will be a back projection of Beauty running in front of trees and a fall backwards which will enhance the flight scene.

I have shot Bérard, Auric and myself for the credits.

At Joinville yesterday I saw a rough edited copy of the complete film which Ibéria has done. It's hard to watch a film like this when it's not permeated by the element of music. I shall have to move some scenes around, alternating the Beast's castle with the Merchant's house and the spring with Diana's pavilion. How good is this film which is drawn from my substance? I wonder. It is too much a part of me, it bristles with too many associations for me to judge of this.

I shall wait for Monday. Perhaps on Monday I'll see things more clearly. I'll begin the editing. After this new montage I shall tackle the details; after the details, the synchronization; after the synchronization, the mixing and the music. I won't show it to Georges Auric until the large errors have been eliminated.

Friday, January 18, 1946.

And here I am in bed again in my little red room. This time it's flu, which attacked me with the suddenness of a tornado. I can't get on with the editing that I was doing in between rehearsals at the Théâtre du Gymnase. I am making corrections, moving things to new places, making deletions and additions over the telephone. A temperature of 104 has left me horribly weak. Outside it is snowing. Inside my head fatigue is circulating like that far-off snow in the glass balls we had as children. Auric's to see the film at two. Darbon and Clément are driving him to Joinville. I am fretting at the Palais-Royal. I'll wait for them to visit me here.

Last Sunday, Gaston P. asked Bérard and me to dine with him at the Ministry of War. We were surprised to find the place transformed by central heating and the treasures of the state furniture collection.

P. wanted us to tell him why the French film industry can't make a go of it. I told him. I don't think he realized things were so bad. Prudence and shrewd dealings keep exact information from reaching those higher up. I hope that my chance journey into this strange universe will serve our country. P., alarmed, asked me to prepare a confidential report. I told him that a report was out of my province, but that I would request one from the department heads, who can do no more than complain without ever getting results.

I have requested reports from Orin (president of the technical commission), Duverger (director of sound at Saint-Maurice) and that perfect sound technician Jacques Lebreton.

Unfortunately, in my opinion, the situation's hopeless, and we'll have to burn the remaining studios and equipment if France is to keep her place when color forces the companies to abandon the barns where we now have to work.

P. spoke of "creating a style." You don't create a style by airing the treasures of the state furniture collection. You create a style by exempting artists from taxes and allowing them to live. In 1946 a painter can't even dream of taking a little country cottage, as the Impressionists did. The more he gains, the more he loses.

M. asked Paul: "Why is Jean making a film? They don't last." An amazing statement. As if anything at all was lasting, beginning with the world!

I am not a person who writes to regular hours. I only write when I cannot do otherwise. And as little as possible. Writing dialogue bores me. But to set in motion this giant dream machine, to wrestle with the angel of light, the angel of machines, the angel of space and time, is a job I am cut out for. The result doesn't much matter. I don't say that what I've done is well done. I've done my best to prove that France can still fight against immense odds—no—that France *can no longer fight except against immense odds*. That is her true task. If France stubbornly denies her privileges and persists in wanting what she can't have and despising what she owes to herself, then we will have only a shroud of royal purple. Let's die and wait for the future to come and pray on our Acropolis.

"Cinema is not an art." Absurd statement. It's being prevented from becoming one. It will only be an art when the silk industrialists stop thinking they're silkworms.

Saturday, January 19th.

In my bed of fever I toss and turn, worrying how I can edit the end of the film so as to avoid a certain weakness of Alekan. This weakness is not his fault. We're all to blame. The trouble was that we had to finish up in such a panic of haste, what with our sets being demolished and other people waiting to come into the studios. We only see our mistakes when we stop. When you're actually shooting the film, there's no pause in the rhythm. The mind never rests or enjoys the least objectivity.

Now I am spending my periods of insomnia understanding my mistakes and thinking up methods of editing so that they won't be so noticeable.

Last night I thought of a way of making the moment of the Prince's appearance more arresting.

After the shock of Avenant's fall in the snow I will cut to Beauty drawing back and crying: "Where is the Beast?" After which, in a full-length shot, I will show the Prince getting up all at once. I shall delete the glove, the hand and the head-and-shoulders shots of the Prince, which lacked vivacity.

Perhaps I'll finish the film with a shot of the snow falling on Avenant as he lies in the pavilion turned into the Beast. I'll see.

Sunday, January 20th.

I think I have awakened feeling better despite pain in my left eye. But I must expect the parts of the machine to go out of order one after the other. Or perhaps the germs are escaping and destroying everything in their path. That is a possibility, too.

Darbon phoned me this morning. We are to lunch at Joinville on Tuesday and synchronize the sisters' scene. On Wednesday I'll go and reedit the end of the picture. It is painful to live knowing that this reel is badly done.

France, truly a collection of *individuals* and unfitted for mobo-cracy, will be a place that only exceptional beings can tolerate—even if they're only exceptional swindlers. Poets will be able to live in France so long as they don't get trapped by positions and honors.

I have the luck of being one of those people who can help to prevent that dance of death. And I hope I shall go on being so (I myself would joyfully die for this priesthood of total liberty). Thus I shall serve France more than those who talk so much about it.

Tuesday the 22nd, 8 a.m.

I went to Saint-Maurice yesterday with Mila, Nane, Michel and Jeannot. I had an injection of Solucamphor in the morning. I didn't feel very tired any more. I like Saint-Maurice and feel quite at home there.

We went into the auditorium after lunch and immediately started work. The job was to put the girls' voices in the mouth of the boys who are imitating them. The reel was run again and again, once with sound, the other times silent. The text was run under the picture. It was easy work, for the boys were imitating the girls who needed only to imitate the boys. I stayed in the control room. Thus I saw the film through a glass pane and heard it through a loudspeaker. It was extremely funny hearing Nane's voice coming from Michel.

After the draper sequence I corrected some of Mila's and Nane's fluffs. We were through at five.

We went to see Raimu working on *L'Eternel Mari*.[67] He has terrific presence.

Watching him on the set, I realized how much physical beauty can handicap an actor and how a face full of expression and character can help him. The "mugs." Katharine Hepburn, whom I saw in a film yesterday evening, is more than beautiful. She has a "mug." A "mug" that catches the light outside and inside. Carved out with a pruning hook or an axe, *with fantastic delicacy*.

Thursday evening, 11 o'clock.

Since yesterday I've had my ears full of that strange foreign—almost Slavic—language of the world going backwards. I've been watching my characters living backwards and hearing them speak that language which resembles a real language because it has the same architecture as ours. It's rough, raucous, aggressive, heavy, turned up at the ends. It issues from the mouths I know so well with amazing fluency. I just have to reverse the handle and they jabber, roar, hesitate and suddenly translate into French their conversation in the unknown language.

Editing a film is one of the most exciting jobs. With a pair of scissors and some glue you can correct the life you've created.

[67] [Working title (which shows its derivation from the Dostoyevski story) of *L'Homme au chapeau rond* (1946), directed by Pierre Billon.]

You add, delete, shift around, synchronize one character's lines with the shot of the character who is listening, jump from one place to another, accelerate a gait, limit a gesture.

Friday evening, 11 o'clock.

My cold seems worse again. I am coughing and blowing my nose all the time and can't sleep. Spent the day at Saint-Maurice. I do like this place, a real village where I have suffered and lived in triplicate. I corrected the first three reels in the morning. Georges Auric was to come at 2:30. I showed them to him after lunch and he took timings with a stop watch. We returned to Paris, where we shut ourselves up in Madame Rolle's office in the Théâtre du Gymnase to talk shop. I'd like a choir, a normal orchestra, and a very strange small orchestra for the Beast's castle.

Having determined the places for these three styles, we went on to the stage, where my play was being rehearsed. Yvonne de Bray is admirable even when she speaks her lines quietly and casually.

February 2, 1946.

For several days I have abandoned Saint-Maurice and the film. With all the cutting and going backwards and forwards in the story, I couldn't see it any more. Everything seemed dull and endless. Auric's working and timing his music.

I had become obsessed by the film, and that is always hateful. I was coughing at night. I dreamt that my cough was a mistake in the editing, and that by cutting, pasting and moving the cough I could sleep quietly. I would wake up and cough and the dream would continue in my half-waking state. I "edited" my cough but couldn't find the right place for it. Dreams like this and the impossibility of working on my poem or even answering my letters made me decide to break with this man-in-the-moon existence. Ibéria has been preparing the reels for synchronization and telephoning me. I have been getting this film out of my system by attending the rehearsals of *Les Parents Terribles*. Madame Rolle and the cast were a little cross with me. They thought I was a prisoner at Joinville.

This morning I am going to the Discina to see Orin about the credits and Alekan about the continuity shots.

February 13, 1946.

I have jaundice. That was all that was missing! I am so run down I must catch any disease that's going round. I already felt very ill yesterday; I had someone drive me to Saint-Maurice so I could finish the cuts. I deleted the long panning shot of Beauty's room as it added nothing to what I show later. I deleted several other shots here and there.

Les Parents Terribles at the Gymnase is having a greater success than we expected, but Marais has a touch of tracheitis and Gabrielle Dorziat has lost her voice. Her understudy is on.

My work's going well. I can leave Paris for a change of air. Darbon is taking me to Haute-Savoie.

If other nations ask France what her armaments are she can reply: "I have none. I have a secret weapon." If asked what that is, she will say that one does not reveal a secret weapon. If they insist, she'll lose nothing by showing her secret because it is inimitable. *It is her tradition of anarchy.*

As soon as people try to organize France and adopt systems, the individual revolts and slips through the gears of their machine. The result is that the swindlers triumph, but another result is a great force expressed in secret, a great spirit of contradiction (which is at the bottom of the spirit of creativity) which escapes the official élites and forms deep-lying élites of its own. For several centuries France has exhibited this rhythm and Frenchmen have continued to say France was decadent.

France is always disparaging herself. I possess a copy of an article written by Musset during the most fertile period where he states that there are no poets, novelists or playwrights, that Madame Malibran sings in London because the Opéra is incapable of singing in tune, and that the Comédie-Française is collapsing under the dust. Corneille as an old man used to buy up the seats in Racine's theater so that he would play to an empty house; Racine's plays were compared unfavorably with the innumerable tragedies then produced; the king employed Molière as a writer of revues to torment his marquesses and doctors. Except for the Encyclopedists, who were the first "men of letters," skillful and ferocious, France usually let its genius perish of poverty.

Who made this notorious grandeur of France which one talks so much about? Villon, Nerval, Baudelaire, Rimbaud, Verlaine.

And we know what happened to those unhappy gentlemen, expelled by society and dying in the hospital or the street.

I find it admirable that France doesn't appreciate herself and runs herself down. For those who think they are poets have a tendency to live poetically; and those who think they are *princes* try to live historically. Both these delusions reduce one to ridicule and are expensive poses to maintain. As Erik Satie used to say: "One cannot both be and seem to be." And he added the phrase which I'm always quoting: "It is not enough to refuse the Légion d'Honneur, the thing is not to have deserved it!"

The film industry opposes an unscalable wall to the *accidental*, the *unforeseen*, the *anarchic*. Pascal[68] saw my film last week. "France is the only country at present where you could possibly make a film like this," he said. Whether it pleases or displeases is another matter. I have been able to complete it, thanks to the willingness of a free producer to take risks, thanks to the kindness of my colleagues, thanks to the ingenuity of the staff, thanks to that tradition of anarchy which still, in our country, permits the intrusion of accident into the midst of order.

April, 1946.

A film is never finished. There's always something to do and though a unit breaks up like mercury, it can't reform in the same manner, which makes it very difficult to do the tidying up. Now you have to gather your unit from the kingdom of shadows, each person leaving a world where yours (the film's) was no more than a memory.

Now to this sad studio in Montmartre occupying one floor of a building of dressing rooms, labs and offices, my coworkers come one after another as if leaving their present life habitats in a dream. Very quickly our old euphoria at being together regains its power and it seems natural to see Marais come in dressed as Prince Charming. He was accompanied by a false Josette Day. She reinforced the element of dream (in which such substitutions are common).

Marais had to jump with this girl from a platform twelve feet high down to a piece of grass. Shot backwards in slow motion from the top of the platform, their fall will give me the image of flight

[68] [Most likely the film producer and director Gabriel Pascal (1894–1954), director of *Major Barbara*.]

I have needed to insert between the shot of the take-off and the final frames of the film. Marais had to jump backwards, which is extremely difficult. He didn't show the least fear. He confessed afterwards that he was afraid of frightening his partner. At the last minute she didn't dare to jump, and we went on shooting nothing at top speed. Finally she screwed up her courage but fell clumsily on her leg and refused to jump again. Marais managed to persuade her. She jumped three times. It was impossible to get a fourth take. Anyhow, I've got all I need.

One final shot: the rose lighting up.

Next day at Saint-Maurice for the sound effects.

Nothing so fascinating as watching a job well done. Rauzenat, the effects man, likes his work and gets a lot of enjoyment out of it. Some sound men produce their effects close to the microphone with their fingers, earth, a twig, matches. Rauzenat works with his hands, feet and mouth. For a galloping horse, he strikes his chest and stomach. Shut up in the sound cabin I hear what I see, and through the window I can make out Rauzenat executing a sort of ritual dance.

Next, at the Montvoisin optical effects lab, I spelled out the instructions for the innumerable masking effects required in Marais's metamorphosis into the Beast. The metamorphosis I've already done isn't satisfactory.

This was the day for the music. I had refused to hear any of it while Georges Auric was composing it. I wanted the full effect to be a surprise. After years of working together I had absolute confidence in what he would turn out.

We recorded from 9 a.m. until five in the Maison de la Chimie. This was the most moving operation of all for me. I repeat, it is only the musical element which will permit the film to soar. Désormière[69] conducted. Jacques Lebreton arranged the players and the choir. The microphone was on a long boom in the center of the hall. Behind the orchestra was the screen with the projection of the film, which the half-light and the makeshift machinery made it very hard to see.

Then came the silence, then the three white flashes announcing the images, then the images, and then the marvel of a synchro-

[69] [Roger Désormière (born 1898, retired 1950), a leading French conductor.]

nization which isn't one, because at my request Georges Auric has avoided the close association of image and music, which will only be brought about by the grace of God.

This new universe worried me, upset me, captivated me. I had, without realizing it, composed a musical background of my own, and the waves of the orchestra were running counter to it. Gradually Auric triumphed over my ridiculous embarrassment. My music made way for his. This music is wedded to the film; it impregnates it, exalts it, consummates it. The Beast's spell puts us to sleep and the spectacle of this penumbra of sound is the dream within our sleep.

I watched, I listened, dreaming as I stood in the cabin where Jacques Lebreton was turning his controls to direct the ship. The choir was badly placed. Lebreton will find the right position tomorrow. He will mingle them in with the orchestra. In two weeks I will record this first attempt again.

What's so astonishing for me, as in my diving suit I watch the amalgam of music and images, is the accidental synchronization whose charm can be ruined if the conductor is ahead or behind by half a second. Sometimes it seizes the image and lifts it up, sometimes it smothers it. What I must do is to make notes at the rehearsals and reproduce the accident by design. Sometimes a burst from the choir envelops a close-up, isolates it and thrusts it toward the spectator. Certain shadings cast gloom on a scene which should express apotheosis, but these scenes are illumined again as soon as the orchestra continues at a quicker tempo.

In *Le Sang d'un Poète* I shifted the musical sequences, which were too close to the images, in order to obtain accidental synchronization. This time I shall respect them but I shall direct them. The result will be a counterpoint; that is, sound and image will not run together both saying the same thing at the same time, neutralizing each other.

I shall give positive emphasis to those creative syncopations which jolt and awaken the imagination, by suppressing the music in certain passages. Thus it will be even more noticeable when it is heard and the silent sequences will not form a void since they contain a music of their own. (The void would have resulted had I asked Auric to decide the cuts.)

Saturday, June 1, 1946.

I am writing these last lines of this diary in the country house where I have just taken refuge from bells of all kinds: doorbells, phone bells and the *Rouge est mis.*

I had decided to escape as soon as the film received its finishing touches. Now yesterday, Friday, I showed it to the studio technicians in the Joinville projection room.

The announcement, written on the blackboard by the projectionists, caused a stir at Saint-Maurice. Benches and chairs had been brought in. Lacombe had changed his shooting schedule so that his unit and artists could attend.

At 6:30 Marlene Dietrich was seated beside me and I tried to get up to say a few words. But the accumulation of all those minutes which had led up to that one paralyzed me and I was almost incapable of speech. I sat watching the film, holding Marlene's hand, crushing it without noticing what I was doing. The film unwound, revolved, sparkled, outside of me, solitary, unfeeling, far-off as a heavenly body. It had killed me. It now rejected me and lived its own life. The only thing I could see in it were the memories attached to every foot of it and the suffering it had caused me. I couldn't believe that others would be able to find a story line in it. I thought they were all immersed in my imaginings.

The reception of this audience of technicians was unforgettable. That was my reward. Whatever happens, I shall never experience again the graciousness of this ceremony organized very simply by this little village whose arts and crafts are the canning of dreams.

Afterward, at ten, I dined at the Palais-Royal with Bérard, Boris, Auric, Jean Marais and Claude Ibéria, and we promised always to work together. May fate not separate us.

beauty and the beast
BY MME. LEPRINCE DE BEAUMONT*

Once upon a time there was a merchant who was very rich. He had six children, three boys and three girls. And as he was a wise man he spared no expense for his children's education, and provided them with all sorts of tutors. His daughters were very beautiful; but the youngest especially excited admiration. As a child she was called nothing but "Little Beauty," so that this name stuck to her, causing her sisters much jealousy. Not only was the youngest more beautiful, but also of a better nature. Her sisters were both very proud because they were rich; they behaved like ladies of fashion, and didn't want to receive the visits of other merchants' daughters; they insisted on the company of people of quality. Every day they went to a ball or a play or on a promenade. They laughed at their younger sister, who spent most of her time reading good books at home. As everyone knew that these girls were very rich, several important merchants asked for their hand in marriage; but the two older sisters replied that they would never marry unless they found a duke, or at least a count. Whereas Beauty (for, as I said, that was what the youngest was called) would thank respectfully those who wished to marry her, but told them that she was too young and wanted to look after her father for a few more years.

Then suddenly the merchant lost all his wealth and nothing remained of his estate but a little country house a good way from the town. Weeping, he told his children that they had to go and live there and that if they all worked like peasants they would manage to survive. The two older daughters replied that they did not wish to leave the town, and that they had suitors who would be only too happy to marry them, even though their fortune was

* Born at Rouen in 1711. Died near Annecy in 1780.

gone. The good young ladies were mistaken; their suitors wouldn't look at them when they were poor. Since no one liked them because of their pride, people said: "They don't deserve to be pitied. It's just as well that they've been taken down a peg. Perhaps the sheep which they now have to tend will appreciate their fine airs!" But at the same time everybody said: "As for Beauty, we're really sorry about her misfortune. She's such a good girl! She used to speak so kindly to poor people. She was so gentle, so respectable!"

And though Beauty was penniless, several gentlemen still continued to court her; but she said she could not possibly abandon her father in his misfortune and that she would follow him to the country to console him and help him work. At first she had been very upset at losing her fortune, but then she said to herself: "No matter how much I cry, my tears won't restore my wealth to me. I must try to be happy without a fortune."

When they were settled in their little country house, the merchant and his three sons spent all their time working the fields. Beauty used to get up at four o'clock in the morning and hasten to clean the house and prepare the family's meals. At first she found it very hard, for she was not used to working like a servant; but in two months' time she became stronger and the work even made her healthier. When her work was finished, she would read, play the harpsichord or sing at the spinning wheel. But her sisters were bored to death; they rose at ten in the morning, strolled about all day, and passed their time bemoaning the loss of their beautiful clothes and gay companions. "Look at our younger sister," they said to each other; "she is so vulgar and stupid that she is satisfied with her unhappy position." The good merchant did not agree with them. For he knew that Beauty was more suited than her sisters to distinguish herself in good company. He admired the virtues of this girl, and especially her patience; for her sisters, not content with letting her do all the housework, insulted her all the time.

The family had been living in solitude for a year, when the merchant received a letter informing him that a vessel on which he had merchandise had just arrived safely. This news went straight to the heads of the two older daughters, who thought that they could finally leave the country, where they were so bored. When they saw their father ready to set out, they asked him to bring them back dresses, fur tippets, headdresses and baubles of every kind.

Beauty didn't ask for anything, for she could see that all the money from the merchandise wouldn't be enough to buy what her sisters wanted.

"Don't you want me to buy you anything?" her father asked her.

"Since you are so kind as to think of me," she replied, "please bring me a rose, for none grow here."

Beauty didn't really want a rose, but she didn't want to cast blame on her sisters' conduct by her example; they would have said that she asked for nothing just to be different. The good man departed, but when he arrived his goods were distrained by his creditors; and after all his efforts had failed, he set off as poor as before. He had only thirty miles to go to reach his house, and was already rejoicing at the thought of seeing his children again. But he had to pass through a great wood before reaching his house, and he lost his way. It was snowing heavily and the wind was so strong that twice he was blown from his horse. As night began to fall, he thought he would either perish from hunger or cold or be eaten by the wolves he could hear howling around him. Suddenly, at the end of a long avenue of trees, he saw a bright light which seemed to be far away. He walked in that direction and discovered that the light came from a great castle, which was fully illuminated. The merchant thanked God for the aid He had sent him and hurried toward the castle; but to his surprise he found no one in the courtyards. His horse, which was following him, saw a large stable that was open and went in; finding hay and oats, the poor animal, which was dying of hunger, attacked the food greedily. The merchant tied it up in the stable and then entered the house, where he could find nobody; but coming to a great hall, he found a good fire and a table loaded with food, laid only for one. As the poor man was soaked to the skin with the rain and snow, he went to dry himself by the fire, saying to himself: "The master of the house, or his servants, will pardon me the liberty I have taken, and they will surely come soon."

He waited for a considerable time, but when eleven o'clock struck and he had still seen nobody, he could no longer resist the pangs of hunger, and took a chicken from the table, which he ate in two mouthfuls, trembling as he did so. He also took several drinks of wine, and then, becoming bolder, left the hall and explored several grand apartments, magnificently furnished. Finally he came to a room which contained a good bed, and, as it was past midnight and he was tired, he decided to close the door and go to bed.

It was ten o'clock in the morning when he awoke, and to his surprise, he found a clean suit in the place of his, which had been ruined. "Assuredly," he said to himself, "this castle belongs to some good fairy who has had pity on my situation." Looking out of the window, he saw no more snow, but arbors of flowers to enchant his sight. He returned to the great hall where he had supped on the previous night, and found a little table laid with a cup of hot chocolate. "Thank you, Madame Fairy," he said aloud, "for being so kind as to think of my breakfast." When the good man had drunk his chocolate, he went out to look for his horse; passing beneath a bower of roses, he remembered that Beauty had asked for one, and he broke off a branch which bore several roses. At that moment he heard a terrible noise, and saw coming toward him a Beast so hideous that he nearly fainted. "How ungrateful you are," said the Beast in a terrible voice. "I saved your life by taking you into my castle, and in return for my hospitality, I find you stealing my roses, which I love better than anything else in the whole world. You must die to expiate this crime. I give you only a quarter of an hour to make your peace with God." The merchant threw himself on his knees and, clasping his hands together, said to the Beast: "My Lord, pardon me; I did not think I was offending you by plucking a rose for one of my daughters, who had asked me for one."

"I am not called My Lord," replied the monster, "but the Beast. I don't like compliments, I like people to say what they think. So don't expect to move me with your flattery. But you said you had daughters. I will forgive you on condition that one of your daughters comes here willingly to die in your place. Do not argue with me; go. And if your daughters refuse to die in your place, swear that you will return in three months."

The good man had no intention of sacrificing one of his daughters to this ugly monster, but he said to himself: "At least I will have the pleasure of embracing them once more." Thus he swore that he would return, and the Beast told him he could leave when he wished. "But," he added, "I do not want you to leave empty-handed. Go back to the room where you slept; there you will find a great empty chest. You may fill it with anything you see, and I will have it carried to your house." At this, the Beast withdrew, and the poor man said to himself: "If I am to die I shall at least have the consolation of leaving my poor children provided for."

He returned to the chamber where he had slept and, finding a great many gold pieces there, he filled the large chest which the Beast had mentioned, closed it, and taking his horse, which he found in the stable, rode away from that palace feeling as sad as he had been happy when he found it the previous evening. His horse now found its own way along one of the forest paths, and within a few hours the good man reached his little house. His children gathered round him, but instead of responding to their kisses, the merchant began to weep as he looked at them. He was holding the branch of roses which he had brought for Beauty; he gave it to her and said: "Beauty, take these roses. They will cost your unhappy father very dear." Whereupon he told his family of his fatal adventure. After this recital, his two older daughters uttered loud cries and heaped insults on Beauty, who was not crying. "See what this little creature's pride has brought us to!" they said. "Why couldn't she have asked for clothing, like us? Oh no, Miss Beauty must always be different. She is going to cause our father's death, and she isn't even weeping."

"What good would that do?" Beauty replied. "Why should I weep for my father's death, since he will not die? As long as the monster is willing to accept one of his daughters, I intend to deliver myself to his fury, and I am very happy, since by dying I will have the joy of saving my father and proving how much I love him."

"No, Sister," her three brothers said, "you will not die. We will find this monster and if we cannot kill him we will perish in the attempt."

"It is useless to try, my children," said the merchant, "for this Beast's power is so great I have no hope of destroying him. I am deeply touched by Beauty's kind heart, but I do not wish to expose her to death. I am old and have only a short time to live; thus I shall be losing only a few years of life, which I regret only for your sakes, my dear children."

"I assure you, Father," said Beauty, "that you shall not go back to that palace without me. You cannot prevent me from following you. I am not greatly attached to life although I am young, and I would rather be devoured by this monster than die of the grief your death would cause me."

Despite all that was said to her, Beauty insisted on departing for the beautiful palace, and her sisters were delighted because the virtues of their younger sister had made them furious with jealousy. The merchant was so occupied with his grief at losing his daughter that he forgot all about the chest he had filled with gold, but as soon as he had shut himself inside his room to go to sleep he was astonished to find it beside his bed. He decided not to tell his children of his new wealth, because his two older daughters would have wanted to return to town, and he was determined to die in the country. But he confided in Beauty, who told him that several gentlemen had called during his absence, two of whom were courting her sisters. She begged her father to give them husbands, for she was so good that she loved them and forgave them with all her heart for the evil they had done her. These wicked girls rubbed their eyes with an onion so that they could cry when Beauty set out with her father, but her brothers wept as genuinely as the merchant. Beauty, alone, did not weep, because she did not wish to add to their grief. The horse took the road to the palace, and by evening they saw it, illuminated as it was the first time. The horse went of its own accord to the stable, and the good man entered the great hall with his daughter. There they found a table, magnificently dressed and laid with two places. The merchant had no desire to eat, but Beauty, forcing herself to appear calm, sat down at the table and served her father; then she said to herself:

"The Beast gives me such good food because he wants to fatten me up before eating me."

When they had supped, they heard a great noise and the merchant, knowing it was the Beast, wept and said farewell to his daughter. When Beauty saw the Beast's hideous face she could not stop herself from shuddering, but she tried to control her fear, and when the monster asked her if she had come willingly, she replied tremblingly that that was so.

"That is good of you," said the Beast, "and I am much obliged. Sir, leave tomorrow morning and never try to return. Good night, Beauty."

"Good night, Beast," she replied, and immediately the monster withdrew.

"Oh my daughter," cried the merchant, embracing Beauty, "I am half dead with fear. Listen to me and leave me here."

"No, Father," said Beauty, with firmness, "you will go tomorrow morning, and leave me in the care of Heaven, which will perhaps have pity on me."

They went to their rooms, thinking that they would not sleep at all, but hardly were they in their beds than their eyes closed. In her slumber Beauty saw a lady who said to her: "I am pleased with your good heart, Beauty. Your good deed of giving up your life to save your father's will not go without reward." When she awoke, Beauty told her father of this dream. Though he consoled her somewhat, he nonetheless uttered loud cries when the time came to part from his beloved daughter.

When he had gone, Beauty sat down in the great hall and began to weep too; but as she had a great deal of courage, she commended herself to God, resolving not to grieve during the little time she had left to live. For she believed firmly that the Beast would devour her that evening. While waiting she decided to go for a walk and explore this beautiful castle. She could not help admiring its grandeur; then, to her surprise, she saw a door, on which was written "Beauty's Apartment." She immediately opened the door and was dazzled by the elegance within. But what pleased her most was a huge bookcase, a harpsichord and several volumes of music. "They don't want me to be bored," she said quietly. Then she thought: "If I were going to stay here for only one day, I wouldn't have been provided for like this."

This thought revived her courage. She opened the bookcase and saw a book on which, in letters of gold, were written these words: "Desire, command; here you are the queen and mistress." "Alas," she sighed, "the only thing I wish is to see my poor father and to know how he is at the moment."

She said that to herself. What was her surprise, as she glanced into a great mirror, to see her home in it, with her father just arriving there, looking extremely sad! Her sisters came out to meet him; and in spite of all the grimaces they made to appear distressed, the joy they felt at the loss of their sister was plainly written on their faces. After a moment, the mirror cleared. Beauty couldn't help thinking that the Beast was very obliging, and that she had nothing to fear. At noon she found the table laid, and while she ate the meal she heard an exquisite concert, although she could not see anyone. In the evening, as she was about to sit down at the table, she again heard the noise the Beast made, and in spite of herself, she shivered with terror.

"Beauty," said the monster, "are you willing to let me watch you sup?"

"You are the master here," she answered, trembling.

"No," replied the Beast, "there is no master here but you. If I trouble you, you have only to tell me to go away, and I shall do so at once. I suppose you find me very ugly, don't you?"

"That is true," said Beauty, "for I cannot lie; but I think that you are very kind."

"You are right," said the Beast; "but not only am I ugly, I am also simple. I know very well I am only a foolish animal."

"You aren't foolish," Beauty replied, "if you say you are, for fools never recognize their stupidity."

"Then eat, Beauty," said the monster, "and try not to be sad in your house; for everything here is yours, and I shall grieve if you are not happy."

"You are very kind," said Beauty. "I must confess that your goodness pleases me, and when I come to think of it, you no longer seem so ugly."

"Yes, Beauty," the Beast replied, "I have a good heart, but I am a monster."

"Many men are more bestial than you," Beauty said, "and I like you with your face better than those who, beneath a man's face, hide a false, corrupt and ungrateful heart."

"If I were not so stupid," he replied, "I would compliment you by way of thanks, but as I am, all I can say is that I am much obliged to you."

Beauty enjoyed her supper, for she hardly feared the monster any more, but she nearly died of fright when he said to her: "Beauty, will you be my wife?" For a long time she made no answer, for she was afraid that her refusal might arouse his wrath. Finally she said, trembling, "No, Beast."

At that moment the poor monster, wanting to sigh, emitted such a horrifying whistling sound that the whole palace echoed. But Beauty was soon reassured, for the Beast said sadly: "Good night, then, Beauty," and left the room, turning around several times to look at her again. Once Beauty was alone, she was overwhelmed with sympathy for this poor Beast. "What a pity," she said, "that he is so ugly, for he is so kind!"

Beauty spent three peaceful months in the castle. Every evening the Beast came to see her and spoke to her during her supper with much good sense, but never with what the world would call wit. Each day Beauty discovered fresh signs of the monster's kindness. From seeing him so often, she had grown accustomed to his ugliness and she no longer feared the moment of his visit; indeed, she often looked at her watch to see if it was almost nine o'clock, for the Beast never failed to appear at that time. The only thing that caused Beauty any distress was that before the monster retired every evening, he always asked her if she would be his wife; and when she refused, he seemed to be in pain. One day she said to him: "You cause me much distress, Beast. I would like to be able to marry you, but I am too sincere to make you believe that that could ever happen. I shall always be your friend; try to content yourself with that."

"I must," replied the Beast, "for in truth I know I am most horrible to look at, though I love you very much; nevertheless, I am happy because you are willing to remain here. Promise me that you will never leave me."

Beauty blushed at these words; for in her mirror she had seen her father pining away at losing her, and she wished to see him again. "I could promise never to leave you altogether; but I am so homesick to see my father that I shall die of grief if you refuse me that pleasure."

"I would rather die myself," said the monster, "than cause you any unhappiness; I shall send you home to your father, you will stay there, and your poor Beast will die of grief."

"No," said Beauty, weeping, "I like you too much to wish to cause your death. I promise to return in a week. You have let me see that my sisters are married, and that my brothers have gone away to join the army. My father is all alone. Allow me to remain with him a week."

"Tomorrow morning you will be there," said the Beast, "but remember your promise. You have only to lay your ring on a table when you go to bed, whenever you want to return. Farewell, Beauty."

With these words he sighed, as he often did, and Beauty went to bed very sad at having saddened him. When she woke up in the morning, she found herself in her father's house. She rang a bell which was beside her bed, and in came the maid, who cried out at seeing her. At this the good merchant ran up to her room and was overwhelmed with joy at the sight of his dear daughter. For more than a quarter of an hour they embraced each other. Beauty, after her first raptures, realized that she had no clothes to go about in, but the maid told her that she had just found a huge chest in the next room full of dresses embroidered with gold and studded with diamonds. Beauty thanked her good Beast for his forethought,

and taking the most modest dress for herself, she told the maid to
store away the rest, which she wished to give to her sisters. As soon
as she said this the chest disappeared. Her father told her that the
Beast wished her to keep the dresses for herself, and no sooner had
he said this than they appeared again in the same spot. While
Beauty dressed, a message was sent to her sisters, who, with their
husbands, came hurrying to the house. They were both very
unhappy. The oldest had married a young gentleman handsome
as Love himself, but he was so much taken with his own face that
he did nothing but admire it from morning till night and had no
time to admire his wife. The second had married a man who had
considerable wit, which he used only to antagonize everyone,
beginning with his wife. Beauty's sisters were nearly consumed
with jealousy when they saw her dressed like a princess and more
radiant than the day. Though she welcomed them with tenderness,
they could not stifle their spite, which became more venomous
as she told them of the happiness she had found. These two jealous
sisters went down into the garden to give full vent to their tears,
and they said to one another:

"Why should that little hussy be happier than we, when we are
so much more lovable than she?"

"Sister," said the oldest, "an idea has occurred to me. Let us try
and keep her here beyond the week. Her stupid Beast will become
angry with her for breaking her promise, and perhaps devour her."

"That's a good idea," replied the other. "To do that, we had best
make a great fuss over her."

With this scheme in mind they immediately went upstairs again
and feigned so much affection toward their sister that Beauty wept
for joy. When the week was nearly over, the two sisters tore their
hair and pretended to be so distraught that she promised to stay
for another week.

Nevertheless, Beauty reproached herself for the unhappiness she
was going to cause her poor Beast, whom she loved with all her
heart, and whom she longed to see again. On the tenth night at her
father's home, she dreamt that she was back in the castle garden,
and that she saw the Beast lying prostrate on the grass about to die,
and reproaching her for her ingratitude. Beauty woke with a start
and burst into tears.

"How wicked I am," she said to herself, "to make a Beast suffer
so when he has been so kind to me. Is it his fault that he is so ugly
and so simple? He is kind, which is better than the rest. Why did I

refuse to marry him? I would be happier with him than my sisters are with their husbands. It is neither good looks nor wit in a husband which makes his wife content; it is goodness of character, virtue and obligingness, and the Beast has all these good qualities. Though I am not in love with him, yet I respect him and feel friendship and gratitude toward him. I must not make him unhappy. If I do, I shall reproach myself with my ingratitude all my life."

With this, she got up, placed her ring on the table and got back to bed. No sooner was she in bed than she fell asleep. When she woke in the morning it was with joy that she found herself back in the Beast's palace. She dressed herself magnificently to please him, and then waited impatiently through the day for nine o'clock; but when the clock struck that hour, the Beast failed to appear. Beauty then feared that she had caused his death. She ran through the palace, uttering loud cries; she was in despair. After searching everywhere, she remembered her dream, and ran through the garden to the stream where she had seen him in her sleep. She found the poor Beast lying unconscious, and she thought he was dead. She threw herself on his body, no longer feeling any revulsion at his appearance. Hearing his heart still beating, she took some water from the stream and sprinkled it on his head.

The Beast opened his eyes and said to Beauty: "You forgot your promise, and my sorrow at losing you made me want to die of hunger; but I die content since I have the pleasure of seeing you once again."

"No, my dear Beast, you shall not die," said Beauty, "you shall live to marry me; for I now give you my hand and swear that I will be yours alone. Alas, I thought it was only friendship that I felt for you, but the grief I feel shows me that I cannot live without seeing you."

No sooner had Beauty said these words than the whole castle lit up; fireworks, music, everything announced a festive occasion. But Beauty paid little attention to these beauties; she turned back to her dear Beast, for whose health she still trembled. To her amazement, the Beast had disappeared and she saw at her feet a prince more beautiful than Love himself, who was thanking her for breaking his spell. Though this prince deserved all her attention she could not help asking where the Beast was.

"You see him at your feet," replied the Prince. "A wicked fairy had doomed me to keep this appearance until a beautiful girl consented to marry me, and she had forbidden me to show my intelligence. Thus no one in the world but you was good enough to be touched by the goodness of my character. Though I offer you my crown I cannot repay the debt I owe you."

Beauty, delightfully surprised, gave her hand to this handsome Prince to raise him up. Together they went inside the castle, and to her great joy, she found her father and all her family in the great hall, where they had been transported by the beautiful lady who had appeared to Beauty in her dream. "Beauty," said this lady, who was a powerful fairy, "come and receive the reward for the good choice you have made. You have preferred virtue to beauty and wit, and you deserve to find all these qualities combined in one person. You will become a great queen; I hope your throne will not destroy your virtues.

"As for you, young ladies," said the fairy to Beauty's two sisters, "I know your hearts and all the malice they contain. Become two statues, yet keep your reason within the stone that shall imprison you. You will remain at the gate of your sister's palace, and I impose no other punishment on you than to witness her happiness. You can return to your former state only when you recognize your own faults; but I'm very much afraid you will always remain statues. People get over pride, bad temper, greediness and sloth, but the conversion of a mean and envious heart is practically a miracle."

At that moment the fairy waved her wand and all those in that hall were transported to the Prince's kingdom. His subjects welcomed him with joy, and he married Beauty, who lived with him a very long time in perfect happiness, because their happiness was founded on virtue.

A CATALOG OF SELECTED
DOVER BOOKS
IN ALL FIELDS OF INTEREST

A CATALOG OF SELECTED DOVER
BOOKS IN ALL FIELDS OF INTEREST

CONCERNING THE SPIRITUAL IN ART, Wassily Kandinsky. Pioneering work by father of abstract art. Thoughts on color theory, nature of art. Analysis of earlier masters. 12 illustrations. 80pp. of text. 5⅜ x 8½.   23411-8 Pa. $4.95

ANIMALS: 1,419 Copyright-Free Illustrations of Mammals, Birds, Fish, Insects, etc., Jim Harter (ed.). Clear wood engravings present, in extremely lifelike poses, over 1,000 species of animals. One of the most extensive pictorial sourcebooks of its kind. Captions. Index. 284pp. 9 x 12.   23766-4 Pa. $14.95

CELTIC ART: The Methods of Construction, George Bain. Simple geometric techniques for making Celtic interlacements, spirals, Kells-type initials, animals, humans, etc. Over 500 illustrations. 160pp. 9 x 12. (USO)   22923-8 Pa. $9.95

AN ATLAS OF ANATOMY FOR ARTISTS, Fritz Schider. Most thorough reference work on art anatomy in the world. Hundreds of illustrations, including selections from works by Vesalius, Leonardo, Goya, Ingres, Michelangelo, others. 593 illustrations. 192pp. 7⅛ x 10¼.   20241-0 Pa. $9.95

CELTIC HAND STROKE-BY-STROKE (Irish Half-Uncial from "The Book of Kells"): An Arthur Baker Calligraphy Manual, Arthur Baker. Complete guide to creating each letter of the alphabet in distinctive Celtic manner. Covers hand position, strokes, pens, inks, paper, more. Illustrated. 48pp. 8¼ x 11.   24336-2 Pa. $3.95

EASY ORIGAMI, John Montroll. Charming collection of 32 projects (hat, cup, pelican, piano, swan, many more) specially designed for the novice origami hobbyist. Clearly illustrated easy-to-follow instructions insure that even beginning papercrafters will achieve successful results. 48pp. 8¼ x 11.   27298-2 Pa. $3.50

THE COMPLETE BOOK OF BIRDHOUSE CONSTRUCTION FOR WOODWORKERS, Scott D. Campbell. Detailed instructions, illustrations, tables. Also data on bird habitat and instinct patterns. Bibliography. 3 tables. 63 illustrations in 15 figures. 48pp. 5¼ x 8½.   24407-5 Pa. $2.50

BLOOMINGDALE'S ILLUSTRATED 1886 CATALOG: Fashions, Dry Goods and Housewares, Bloomingdale Brothers. Famed merchants' extremely rare catalog depicting about 1,700 products: clothing, housewares, firearms, dry goods, jewelry, more. Invaluable for dating, identifying vintage items. Also, copyright-free graphics for artists, designers. Co-published with Henry Ford Museum & Greenfield Village. 160pp. 8¼ x 11.   25780-0 Pa. $10.95

HISTORIC COSTUME IN PICTURES, Braun & Schneider. Over 1,450 costumed figures in clearly detailed engravings—from dawn of civilization to end of 19th century. Captions. Many folk costumes. 256pp. 8⅜ x 11¾.   23150-X Pa. $12.95

STICKLEY CRAFTSMAN FURNITURE CATALOGS, Gustav Stickley and L. & J. G. Stickley. Beautiful, functional furniture in two authentic catalogs from 1910. 594 illustrations, including 277 photos, show settles, rockers, armchairs, reclining chairs, bookcases, desks, tables. 183pp. 6½ x 9¼. 23838-5 Pa. $11.95

AMERICAN LOCOMOTIVES IN HISTORIC PHOTOGRAPHS: 1858 to 1949, Ron Ziel (ed.). A rare collection of 126 meticulously detailed official photographs, called "builder portraits," of American locomotives that majestically chronicle the rise of steam locomotive power in America. Introduction. Detailed captions. xi + 129pp. 9 x 12. 27393-8 Pa. $13.95

AMERICA'S LIGHTHOUSES: An Illustrated History, Francis Ross Holland, Jr. Delightfully written, profusely illustrated fact-filled survey of over 200 American lighthouses since 1716. History, anecdotes, technological advances, more. 240pp. 8 x 10¾. 25576-X Pa. $12.95

TOWARDS A NEW ARCHITECTURE, Le Corbusier. Pioneering manifesto by founder of "International School." Technical and aesthetic theories, views of industry, economics, relation of form to function, "mass-production split" and much more. Profusely illustrated. 320pp. 6⅛ x 9¼. (USO) 25023-7 Pa. $9.95

HOW THE OTHER HALF LIVES, Jacob Riis. Famous journalistic record, exposing poverty and degradation of New York slums around 1900, by major social reformer. 100 striking and influential photographs. 233pp. 10 x 7⅞. 22012-5 Pa. $11.95

FRUIT KEY AND TWIG KEY TO TREES AND SHRUBS, William M. Harlow. One of the handiest and most widely used identification aids. Fruit key covers 120 deciduous and evergreen species; twig key 160 deciduous species. Easily used. Over 300 photographs. 126pp. 5⅜ x 8½. 20511-8 Pa. $3.95

COMMON BIRD SONGS, Dr. Donald J. Borror. Songs of 60 most common U.S. birds: robins, sparrows, cardinals, bluejays, finches, more—arranged in order of increasing complexity. Up to 9 variations of songs of each species. Cassette and manual 99911-4 $8.95

ORCHIDS AS HOUSE PLANTS, Rebecca Tyson Northen. Grow cattleyas and many other kinds of orchids—in a window, in a case, or under artificial light. 63 illustrations. 148pp. 5⅜ x 8½. 23261-1 Pa. $5.95

MONSTER MAZES, Dave Phillips. Masterful mazes at four levels of difficulty. Avoid deadly perils and evil creatures to find magical treasures. Solutions for all 32 exciting illustrated puzzles. 48pp. 8¼ x 11. 26005-4 Pa. $2.95

MOZART'S DON GIOVANNI (DOVER OPERA LIBRETTO SERIES), Wolfgang Amadeus Mozart. Introduced and translated by Ellen H. Bleiler. Standard Italian libretto, with complete English translation. Convenient and thoroughly portable—an ideal companion for reading along with a recording or the performance itself. Introduction. List of characters. Plot summary. 121pp. 5¼ x 8½. 24944-1 Pa. $3.95

TECHNICAL MANUAL AND DICTIONARY OF CLASSICAL BALLET, Gail Grant. Defines, explains, comments on steps, movements, poses and concepts. 15-page pictorial section. Basic book for student, viewer. 127pp. 5⅜ x 8½. 21843-0 Pa. $4.95

CATALOG OF DOVER BOOKS

THE CLARINET AND CLARINET PLAYING, David Pino. Lively, comprehensive work features suggestions about technique, musicianship, and musical interpretation, as well as guidelines for teaching, making your own reeds, and preparing for public performance. Includes an intriguing look at clarinet history. "A godsend," The Clarinet, Journal of the International Clarinet Society. Appendixes. 7 illus. 320pp. 5⅜ x 8½. 40270-3 Pa. $9.95

HOLLYWOOD GLAMOR PORTRAITS, John Kobal (ed.). 145 photos from 1926-49. Harlow, Gable, Bogart, Bacall; 94 stars in all. Full background on photographers, technical aspects. 160pp. 8⅜ x 11¼. 23352-9 Pa. $12.95

THE ANNOTATED CASEY AT THE BAT: A Collection of Ballads about the Mighty Casey/Third, Revised Edition, Martin Gardner (ed.). Amusing sequels and parodies of one of America's best-loved poems: Casey's Revenge, Why Casey Whiffed, Casey's Sister at the Bat, others. 256pp. 5⅜ x 8½. 28598-7 Pa. $8.95

THE RAVEN AND OTHER FAVORITE POEMS, Edgar Allan Poe. Over 40 of the author's most memorable poems: "The Bells," "Ulalume," "Israfel," "To Helen," "The Conqueror Worm," "Eldorado," "Annabel Lee," many more. Alphabetic lists of titles and first lines. 64pp. 5³⁄₁₆ x 8¼. 26685-0 Pa. $1.00

PERSONAL MEMOIRS OF U. S. GRANT, Ulysses Simpson Grant. Intelligent, deeply moving firsthand account of Civil War campaigns, considered by many the finest military memoirs ever written. Includes letters, historic photographs, maps and more. 528pp. 6⅛ x 9¼. 28587-1 Pa. $12.95

ANCIENT EGYPTIAN MATERIALS AND INDUSTRIES, A. Lucas and J. Harris. Fascinating, comprehensive, thoroughly documented text describes this ancient civilization's vast resources and the processes that incorporated them in daily life, including the use of animal products, building materials, cosmetics, perfumes and incense, fibers, glazed ware, glass and its manufacture, materials used in the mummification process, and much more. 544pp. 6¹⁄₈ x 9¼. (USO) 40446-3 Pa. $16.95

RUSSIAN STORIES/PYCCKNE PACCKA3bl: A Dual-Language Book, edited by Gleb Struve. Twelve tales by such masters as Chekhov, Tolstoy, Dostoevsky, Pushkin, others. Excellent word-for-word English translations on facing pages, plus teaching and study aids, Russian/English vocabulary, biographical/critical introductions, more. 416pp. 5⅜ x 8½. 26244-8 Pa. $9.95

PHILADELPHIA THEN AND NOW: 60 Sites Photographed in the Past and Present, Kenneth Finkel and Susan Oyama. Rare photographs of City Hall, Logan Square, Independence Hall, Betsy Ross House, other landmarks juxtaposed with contemporary views. Captures changing face of historic city. Introduction. Captions. 128pp. 8¼ x 11. 25790-8 Pa. $9.95

AIA ARCHITECTURAL GUIDE TO NASSAU AND SUFFOLK COUNTIES, LONG ISLAND, The American Institute of Architects, Long Island Chapter, and the Society for the Preservation of Long Island Antiquities. Comprehensive, well-researched and generously illustrated volume brings to life over three centuries of Long Island's great architectural heritage. More than 240 photographs with authoritative, extensively detailed captions. 176pp. 8¼ x 11. 26946-9 Pa. $14.95

NORTH AMERICAN INDIAN LIFE: Customs and Traditions of 23 Tribes, Elsie Clews Parsons (ed.). 27 fictionalized essays by noted anthropologists examine religion, customs, government, additional facets of life among the Winnebago, Crow, Zuni, Eskimo, other tribes. 480pp. 6⅛ x 9¼. 27377-6 Pa. $10.95

CATALOG OF DOVER BOOKS

FRANK LLOYD WRIGHT'S DANA HOUSE, Donald Hoffmann. Pictorial essay of residential masterpiece with over 160 interior and exterior photos, plans, elevations, sketches and studies. 128pp. 9¼ x 10¾. 29120-0 Pa. $12.95

THE MALE AND FEMALE FIGURE IN MOTION: 60 Classic Photographic Sequences, Eadweard Muybridge. 60 true-action photographs of men and women walking, running, climbing, bending, turning, etc., reproduced from rare 19th-century masterpiece. vi + 121pp. 9 x 12. 24745-7 Pa. $10.95

1001 QUESTIONS ANSWERED ABOUT THE SEASHORE, N. J. Berrill and Jacquelyn Berrill. Queries answered about dolphins, sea snails, sponges, starfish, fishes, shore birds, many others. Covers appearance, breeding, growth, feeding, much more. 305pp. 5¼ x 8¼. 23366-9 Pa. $9.95

ATTRACTING BIRDS TO YOUR YARD, William J. Weber. Easy-to-follow guide offers advice on how to attract the greatest diversity of birds: birdhouses, feeders, water and waterers, much more. 96pp. 5³⁄₁₆ x 8¼. 28927-3 Pa. $2.50

MEDICINAL AND OTHER USES OF NORTH AMERICAN PLANTS: A Historical Survey with Special Reference to the Eastern Indian Tribes, Charlotte Erichsen-Brown. Chronological historical citations document 500 years of usage of plants, trees, shrubs native to eastern Canada, northeastern U.S. Also complete identifying information. 343 illustrations. 544pp. 6½ x 9¼. 25951-X Pa. $12.95

STORYBOOK MAZES, Dave Phillips. 23 stories and mazes on two-page spreads: Wizard of Oz, Treasure Island, Robin Hood, etc. Solutions. 64pp. 8¼ x 11. 23628-5 Pa. $2.95

AMERICAN NEGRO SONGS: 230 Folk Songs and Spirituals, Religious and Secular, John W. Work. This authoritative study traces the African influences of songs sung and played by black Americans at work, in church, and as entertainment. The author discusses the lyric significance of such songs as "Swing Low, Sweet Chariot," "John Henry," and others and offers the words and music for 230 songs. Bibliography. Index of Song Titles. 272pp. 6½ x 9¼. 40271-1 Pa. $9.95

MOVIE-STAR PORTRAITS OF THE FORTIES, John Kobal (ed.). 163 glamor, studio photos of 106 stars of the 1940s: Rita Hayworth, Ava Gardner, Marlon Brando, Clark Gable, many more. 176pp. 8⅜ x 11¼. 23546-7 Pa. $14.95

BENCHLEY LOST AND FOUND, Robert Benchley. Finest humor from early 30s, about pet peeves, child psychologists, post office and others. Mostly unavailable elsewhere. 73 illustrations by Peter Arno and others. 183pp. 5⅜ x 8½. 22410-4 Pa. $6.95

YEKL and THE IMPORTED BRIDEGROOM AND OTHER STORIES OF YIDDISH NEW YORK, Abraham Cahan. Film Hester Street based on Yekl (1896). Novel, other stories among first about Jewish immigrants on N.Y.'s East Side. 240pp. 5⅜ x 8½. 22427-9 Pa. $6.95

SELECTED POEMS, Walt Whitman. Generous sampling from *Leaves of Grass*. Twenty-four poems include "I Hear America Singing," "Song of the Open Road," "I Sing the Body Electric," "When Lilacs Last in the Dooryard Bloom'd," "O Captain! My Captain!"—all reprinted from an authoritative edition. Lists of titles and first lines. 128pp. 5³⁄₁₆ x 8¼. 26878-0 Pa. $1.00

THE BEST TALES OF HOFFMANN, E. T. A. Hoffmann. 10 of Hoffmann's most important stories: "Nutcracker and the King of Mice," "The Golden Flowerpot," etc. 458pp. 5⅜ x 8½. 21793-0 Pa. $9.95

FROM FETISH TO GOD IN ANCIENT EGYPT, E. A. Wallis Budge. Rich detailed survey of Egyptian conception of "God" and gods, magic, cult of animals, Osiris, more. Also, superb English translations of hymns and legends. 240 illustrations. 545pp. 5⅜ x 8½. 25803-3 Pa. $13.95

FRENCH STORIES/CONTES FRANÇAIS: A Dual-Language Book, Wallace Fowlie. Ten stories by French masters, Voltaire to Camus: "Micromegas" by Voltaire; "The Atheist's Mass" by Balzac; "Minuet" by de Maupassant; "The Guest" by Camus, six more. Excellent English translations on facing pages. Also French-English vocabulary list, exercises, more. 352pp. 5⅜ x 8½. 26443-2 Pa. $9.95

CHICAGO AT THE TURN OF THE CENTURY IN PHOTOGRAPHS: 122 Historic Views from the Collections of the Chicago Historical Society, Larry A. Viskochil. Rare large-format prints offer detailed views of City Hall, State Street, the Loop, Hull House, Union Station, many other landmarks, circa 1904-1913. Introduction. Captions. Maps. 144pp. 9⅜ x 12¼. 24656-6 Pa. $12.95

OLD BROOKLYN IN EARLY PHOTOGRAPHS, 1865-1929, William Lee Younger. Luna Park, Gravesend race track, construction of Grand Army Plaza, moving of Hotel Brighton, etc. 157 previously unpublished photographs. 165pp. 8⅞ x 11¾. 23587-4 Pa. $13.95

THE MYTHS OF THE NORTH AMERICAN INDIANS, Lewis Spence. Rich anthology of the myths and legends of the Algonquins, Iroquois, Pawnees and Sioux, prefaced by an extensive historical and ethnological commentary. 36 illustrations. 480pp. 5⅜ x 8½. 25967-6 Pa. $10.95

AN ENCYCLOPEDIA OF BATTLES: Accounts of Over 1,560 Battles from 1479 B.C. to the Present, David Eggenberger. Essential details of every major battle in recorded history from the first battle of Megiddo in 1479 B.C. to Grenada in 1984. List of Battle Maps. New Appendix covering the years 1967-1984. Index. 99 illustrations. 544pp. 6½ x 9¼. 24913-1 Pa. $16.95

SAILING ALONE AROUND THE WORLD, Captain Joshua Slocum. First man to sail around the world, alone, in small boat. One of great feats of seamanship told in delightful manner. 67 illustrations. 294pp. 5⅜ x 8½. 20326-3 Pa. $6.95

ANARCHISM AND OTHER ESSAYS, Emma Goldman. Powerful, penetrating, prophetic essays on direct action, role of minorities, prison reform, puritan hypocrisy, violence, etc. 271pp. 5⅜ x 8½. 22484-8 Pa. $7.95

MYTHS OF THE HINDUS AND BUDDHISTS, Ananda K. Coomaraswamy and Sister Nivedita. Great stories of the epics; deeds of Krishna, Shiva, taken from puranas, Vedas, folk tales; etc. 32 illustrations. 400pp. 5⅜ x 8½. 21759-0 Pa. $12.95

THE TRAUMA OF BIRTH, Otto Rank. Rank's controversial thesis that anxiety neurosis is caused by profound psychological trauma which occurs at birth. 256pp. 5⅜ x 8½. 27974-X Pa. $7.95

A THEOLOGICO-POLITICAL TREATISE, Benedict Spinoza. Also contains unfinished Political Treatise. Great classic on religious liberty, theory of government on common consent. R. Elwes translation. Total of 421pp. 5⅜ x 8½. 20249-6 Pa. $9.95

CATALOG OF DOVER BOOKS

MY BONDAGE AND MY FREEDOM, Frederick Douglass. Born a slave, Douglass became outspoken force in antislavery movement. The best of Douglass' autobiographies. Graphic description of slave life. 464pp. 5⅜ x 8½. 22457-0 Pa. $8.95

FOLLOWING THE EQUATOR: A Journey Around the World, Mark Twain. Fascinating humorous account of 1897 voyage to Hawaii, Australia, India, New Zealand, etc. Ironic, bemused reports on peoples, customs, climate, flora and fauna, politics, much more. 197 illustrations. 720pp. 5⅜ x 8½. 26113-1 Pa. $15.95

THE PEOPLE CALLED SHAKERS, Edward D. Andrews. Definitive study of Shakers: origins, beliefs, practices, dances, social organization, furniture and crafts, etc. 33 illustrations. 351pp. 5⅜ x 8½. 21081-2 Pa. $8.95

THE MYTHS OF GREECE AND ROME, H. A. Guerber. A classic of mythology, generously illustrated, long prized for its simple, graphic, accurate retelling of the principal myths of Greece and Rome, and for its commentary on their origins and significance. With 64 illustrations by Michelangelo, Raphael, Titian, Rubens, Canova, Bernini and others. 480pp. 5⅜ x 8½. 27584-1 Pa. $9.95

PSYCHOLOGY OF MUSIC, Carl E. Seashore. Classic work discusses music as a medium from psychological viewpoint. Clear treatment of physical acoustics, auditory apparatus, sound perception, development of musical skills, nature of musical feeling, host of other topics. 88 figures. 408pp. 5⅜ x 8½. 21851-1 Pa. $11.95

THE PHILOSOPHY OF HISTORY, Georg W. Hegel. Great classic of Western thought develops concept that history is not chance but rational process, the evolution of freedom. 457pp. 5⅜ x 8½. 20112-0 Pa. $9.95

THE BOOK OF TEA, Kakuzo Okakura. Minor classic of the Orient: entertaining, charming explanation, interpretation of traditional Japanese culture in terms of tea ceremony. 94pp. 5⅜ x 8½. 20070-1 Pa. $3.95

LIFE IN ANCIENT EGYPT, Adolf Erman. Fullest, most thorough, detailed older account with much not in more recent books, domestic life, religion, magic, medicine, commerce, much more. Many illustrations reproduce tomb paintings, carvings, hieroglyphs, etc. 597pp. 5⅜ x 8½. 22632-8 Pa. $12.95

SUNDIALS, Their Theory and Construction, Albert Waugh. Far and away the best, most thorough coverage of ideas, mathematics concerned, types, construction, adjusting anywhere. Simple, nontechnical treatment allows even children to build several of these dials. Over 100 illustrations. 230pp. 5⅜ x 8½. 22947-5 Pa. $8.95

THEORETICAL HYDRODYNAMICS, L. M. Milne-Thomson. Classic exposition of the mathematical theory of fluid motion, applicable to both hydrodynamics and aerodynamics. Over 600 exercises. 768pp. 6⅛ x 9¼. 68970-0 Pa. $20.95

SONGS OF EXPERIENCE: Facsimile Reproduction with 26 Plates in Full Color, William Blake. 26 full-color plates from a rare 1826 edition. Includes "TheTyger," "London," "Holy Thursday," and other poems. Printed text of poems. 48pp. 5¼ x 7. 24636-1 Pa. $4.95

OLD-TIME VIGNETTES IN FULL COLOR, Carol Belanger Grafton (ed.). Over 390 charming, often sentimental illustrations, selected from archives of Victorian graphics—pretty women posing, children playing, food, flowers, kittens and puppies, smiling cherubs, birds and butterflies, much more. All copyright-free. 48pp. 9¼ x 12¼. 27269-9 Pa. $7.95

PERSPECTIVE FOR ARTISTS, Rex Vicat Cole. Depth, perspective of sky and sea, shadows, much more, not usually covered. 391 diagrams, 81 reproductions of drawings and paintings. 279pp. 5⅜ x 8½. 22487-2 Pa. $7.95

DRAWING THE LIVING FIGURE, Joseph Sheppard. Innovative approach to artistic anatomy focuses on specifics of surface anatomy, rather than muscles and bones. Over 170 drawings of live models in front, back and side views, and in widely varying poses. Accompanying diagrams. 177 illustrations. Introduction. Index. 144pp. 8⅜ x11¼. 26723-7 Pa. $8.95

GOTHIC AND OLD ENGLISH ALPHABETS: 100 Complete Fonts, Dan X. Solo. Add power, elegance to posters, signs, other graphics with 100 stunning copyright-free alphabets: Blackstone, Dolbey, Germania, 97 more—including many lower-case, numerals, punctuation marks. 104pp. 8⅛ x 11. 24695-7 Pa. $8.95

HOW TO DO BEADWORK, Mary White. Fundamental book on craft from simple projects to five-bead chains and woven works. 106 illustrations. 142pp. 5⅜ x 8. 20697-1 Pa. $5.95

THE BOOK OF WOOD CARVING, Charles Marshall Sayers. Finest book for beginners discusses fundamentals and offers 34 designs. "Absolutely first rate . . . well thought out and well executed."—E. J. Tangerman. 118pp. 7¾ x 10⅝. 23654-4 Pa. $7.95

ILLUSTRATED CATALOG OF CIVIL WAR MILITARY GOODS: Union Army Weapons, Insignia, Uniform Accessories, and Other Equipment, Schuyler, Hartley, and Graham. Rare, profusely illustrated 1846 catalog includes Union Army uniform and dress regulations, arms and ammunition, coats, insignia, flags, swords, rifles, etc. 226 illustrations. 160pp. 9 x 12. 24939-5 Pa. $10.95

WOMEN'S FASHIONS OF THE EARLY 1900s: An Unabridged Republication of "New York Fashions, 1909," National Cloak & Suit Co. Rare catalog of mail-order fashions documents women's and children's clothing styles shortly after the turn of the century. Captions offer full descriptions, prices. Invaluable resource for fashion, costume historians. Approximately 725 illustrations. 128pp. 8⅜ x 11¼. 27276-1 Pa. $11.95

THE 1912 AND 1915 GUSTAV STICKLEY FURNITURE CATALOGS, Gustav Stickley. With over 200 detailed illustrations and descriptions, these two catalogs are essential reading and reference materials and identification guides for Stickley furniture. Captions cite materials, dimensions and prices. 112pp. 6½ x 9¼. 26676-1 Pa. $9.95

EARLY AMERICAN LOCOMOTIVES, John H. White, Jr. Finest locomotive engravings from early 19th century: historical (1804–74), main-line (after 1870), special, foreign, etc. 147 plates. 142pp. 11⅜ x 8¼. 22772-3 Pa. $10.95

THE TALL SHIPS OF TODAY IN PHOTOGRAPHS, Frank O. Braynard. Lavishly illustrated tribute to nearly 100 majestic contemporary sailing vessels: Amerigo Vespucci, Clearwater, Constitution, Eagle, Mayflower, Sea Cloud, Victory, many more. Authoritative captions provide statistics, background on each ship. 190 black-and-white photographs and illustrations. Introduction. 128pp. 8⅞ x 11¾. 27163-3 Pa. $14.95

CATALOG OF DOVER BOOKS

LITTLE BOOK OF EARLY AMERICAN CRAFTS AND TRADES, Peter Stockham (ed.). 1807 children's book explains crafts and trades: baker, hatter, cooper, potter, and many others. 23 copperplate illustrations. 140pp. 4⅝ x 6.
23336-7 Pa. $4.95

VICTORIAN FASHIONS AND COSTUMES FROM HARPER'S BAZAR, 1867–1898, Stella Blum (ed.). Day costumes, evening wear, sports clothes, shoes, hats, other accessories in over 1,000 detailed engravings. 320pp. 9⅜ x 12¼.
22990-4 Pa. $15.95

GUSTAV STICKLEY, THE CRAFTSMAN, Mary Ann Smith. Superb study surveys broad scope of Stickley's achievement, especially in architecture. Design philosophy, rise and fall of the Craftsman empire, descriptions and floor plans for many Craftsman houses, more. 86 black-and-white halftones. 31 line illustrations. Introduction 208pp. 6½ x 9¼.
27210-9 Pa. $9.95

THE LONG ISLAND RAIL ROAD IN EARLY PHOTOGRAPHS, Ron Ziel. Over 220 rare photos, informative text document origin (1844) and development of rail service on Long Island. Vintage views of early trains, locomotives, stations, passengers, crews, much more. Captions. 8⅞ x 11¾.
26301-0 Pa. $13.95

VOYAGE OF THE LIBERDADE, Joshua Slocum. Great 19th-century mariner's thrilling, first-hand account of the wreck of his ship off South America, the 35-foot boat he built from the wreckage, and its remarkable voyage home. 128pp. 5⅜ x 8½.
40022-0 Pa. $4.95

TEN BOOKS ON ARCHITECTURE, Vitruvius. The most important book ever written on architecture. Early Roman aesthetics, technology, classical orders, site selection, all other aspects. Morgan translation. 331pp. 5⅜ x 8½. 20645-9 Pa. $8.95

THE HUMAN FIGURE IN MOTION, Eadweard Muybridge. More than 4,500 stopped-action photos, in action series, showing undraped men, women, children jumping, lying down, throwing, sitting, wrestling, carrying, etc. 390pp. 7⅞ x 10⅝.
20204-6 Clothbd. $27.95

TREES OF THE EASTERN AND CENTRAL UNITED STATES AND CANADA, William M. Harlow. Best one-volume guide to 140 trees. Full descriptions, woodlore, range, etc. Over 600 illustrations. Handy size. 288pp. 4½ x 6⅜.
20395-6 Pa. $6.95

SONGS OF WESTERN BIRDS, Dr. Donald J. Borror. Complete song and call repertoire of 60 western species, including flycatchers, juncoes, cactus wrens, many more–includes fully illustrated booklet. Cassette and manual 99913-0 $8.95

GROWING AND USING HERBS AND SPICES, Milo Miloradovich. Versatile handbook provides all the information needed for cultivation and use of all the herbs and spices available in North America. 4 illustrations. Index. Glossary. 236pp. 5⅜ x 8½.
25058-X Pa. $7.95

BIG BOOK OF MAZES AND LABYRINTHS, Walter Shepherd. 50 mazes and labyrinths in all–classical, solid, ripple, and more–in one great volume. Perfect inexpensive puzzler for clever youngsters. Full solutions. 112pp. 8⅛ x 11.
22951-3 Pa. $5.95

PIANO TUNING, J. Cree Fischer. Clearest, best book for beginner, amateur. Simple repairs, raising dropped notes, tuning by easy method of flattened fifths. No previous skills needed. 4 illustrations. 201pp. 5⅜ x 8½. 23267-0 Pa. $6.95

HINTS TO SINGERS, Lillian Nordica. Selecting the right teacher, developing confidence, overcoming stage fright, and many other important skills receive thoughtful discussion in this indispensible guide, written by a world-famous diva of four decades' experience. 96pp. 5³/₈ x 8¹/₂. 40094-8 Pa. $4.95

THE COMPLETE NONSENSE OF EDWARD LEAR, Edward Lear. All nonsense limericks, zany alphabets, Owl and Pussycat, songs, nonsense botany, etc., illustrated by Lear. Total of 320pp. 5⅜ x 8½. (USO) 20167-8 Pa. $7.95

VICTORIAN PARLOUR POETRY: An Annotated Anthology, Michael R. Turner. 117 gems by Longfellow, Tennyson, Browning, many lesser-known poets. "The Village Blacksmith," "Curfew Must Not Ring Tonight," "Only a Baby Small," dozens more, often difficult to find elsewhere. Index of poets, titles, first lines. xxiii + 325pp. 5⅝ x 8¼. 27044-0 Pa. $8.95

DUBLINERS, James Joyce. Fifteen stories offer vivid, tightly focused observations of the lives of Dublin's poorer classes. At least one, "The Dead," is considered a masterpiece. Reprinted complete and unabridged from standard edition. 160pp. 5³⁄₁₆ x 8¼. 26870-5 Pa. $1.00

GREAT WEIRD TALES: 14 Stories by Lovecraft, Blackwood, Machen and Others, S. T. Joshi (ed.). 14 spellbinding tales, including "The Sin Eater," by Fiona McLeod, "The Eye Above the Mantel," by Frank Belknap Long, as well as renowned works by R. H. Barlow, Lord Dunsany, Arthur Machen, W. C. Morrow and eight other masters of the genre. 256pp. 5⅜ x 8½. (USO) 40436-6 Pa. $8.95

THE BOOK OF THE SACRED MAGIC OF ABRAMELIN THE MAGE, translated by S. MacGregor Mathers. Medieval manuscript of ceremonial magic. Basic document in Aleister Crowley, Golden Dawn groups. 268pp. 5⅜ x 8½. 23211-5 Pa. $9.95

NEW RUSSIAN-ENGLISH AND ENGLISH-RUSSIAN DICTIONARY, M. A. O'Brien. This is a remarkably handy Russian dictionary, containing a surprising amount of information, including over 70,000 entries. 366pp. 4½ x 6⅛. 20208-9 Pa. $10.95

HISTORIC HOMES OF THE AMERICAN PRESIDENTS, Second, Revised Edition, Irvin Haas. A traveler's guide to American Presidential homes, most open to the public, depicting and describing homes occupied by every American President from George Washington to George Bush. With visiting hours, admission charges, travel routes. 175 photographs. Index. 160pp. 8¼ x 11. 26751-2 Pa. $11.95

NEW YORK IN THE FORTIES, Andreas Feininger. 162 brilliant photographs by the well-known photographer, formerly with *Life* magazine. Commuters, shoppers, Times Square at night, much else from city at its peak. Captions by John von Hartz. 181pp. 9¼ x 10¾. 23585-8 Pa. $13.95

INDIAN SIGN LANGUAGE, William Tomkins. Over 525 signs developed by Sioux and other tribes. Written instructions and diagrams. Also 290 pictographs. 111pp. 6⅛ x 9¼. 22029-X Pa. $3.95

ANATOMY: A Complete Guide for Artists, Joseph Sheppard. A master of figure drawing shows artists how to render human anatomy convincingly. Over 460 illustrations. 224pp. 8⅜ x 11¼. 27279-6 Pa. $11.95

MEDIEVAL CALLIGRAPHY: Its History and Technique, Marc Drogin. Spirited history, comprehensive instruction manual covers 13 styles (ca. 4th century thru 15th). Excellent photographs; directions for duplicating medieval techniques with modern tools. 224pp. 8⅜ x 11¼. 26142-5 Pa. $12.95

DRIED FLOWERS: How to Prepare Them, Sarah Whitlock and Martha Rankin. Complete instructions on how to use silica gel, meal and borax, perlite aggregate, sand and borax, glycerine and water to create attractive permanent flower arrangements. 12 illustrations. 32pp. 5⅜ x 8½. 21802-3 Pa. $1.00

EASY-TO-MAKE BIRD FEEDERS FOR WOODWORKERS, Scott D. Campbell. Detailed, simple-to-use guide for designing, constructing, caring for and using feeders. Text, illustrations for 12 classic and contemporary designs. 96pp. 5⅜ x 8½. 25847-5 Pa. $3.95

SCOTTISH WONDER TALES FROM MYTH AND LEGEND, Donald A. Mackenzie. 16 lively tales tell of giants rumbling down mountainsides, of a magic wand that turns stone pillars into warriors, of gods and goddesses, evil hags, powerful forces and more. 240pp. 5⅜ x 8½. 29677-6 Pa. $6.95

THE HISTORY OF UNDERCLOTHES, C. Willett Cunnington and Phyllis Cunnington. Fascinating, well-documented survey covering six centuries of English undergarments, enhanced with over 100 illustrations: 12th-century laced-up bodice, footed long drawers (1795), 19th-century bustles, 19th-century corsets for men, Victorian "bust improvers," much more. 272pp. 5⅝ x 8¼. 27124-2 Pa. $9.95

ARTS AND CRAFTS FURNITURE: The Complete Brooks Catalog of 1912, Brooks Manufacturing Co. Photos and detailed descriptions of more than 150 now very collectible furniture designs from the Arts and Crafts movement depict davenports, settees, buffets, desks, tables, chairs, bedsteads, dressers and more, all built of solid, quarter-sawed oak. Invaluable for students and enthusiasts of antiques, Americana and the decorative arts. 80pp. 6½ x 9¼. 27471-3 Pa. $8.95

WILBUR AND ORVILLE: A Biography of the Wright Brothers, Fred Howard. Definitive, crisply written study tells the full story of the brothers' lives and work. A vividly written biography, unparalleled in scope and color, that also captures the spirit of an extraordinary era. 560pp. 6⅛ x 9¼. 40297-5 Pa. $17.95

THE ARTS OF THE SAILOR: Knotting, Splicing and Ropework, Hervey Garrett Smith. Indispensable shipboard reference covers tools, basic knots and useful hitches; handsewing and canvas work, more. Over 100 illustrations. Delightful reading for sea lovers. 256pp. 5⅜ x 8½. 26440-8 Pa. $8.95

FRANK LLOYD WRIGHT'S FALLINGWATER: The House and Its History, Second, Revised Edition, Donald Hoffmann. A total revision–both in text and illustrations–of the standard document on Fallingwater, the boldest, most personal architectural statement of Wright's mature years, updated with valuable new material from the recently opened Frank Lloyd Wright Archives. "Fascinating"–*The New York Times*. 116 illustrations. 128pp. 9¼ x 10¾. 27430-6 Pa. $12.95

CATALOG OF DOVER BOOKS

PHOTOGRAPHIC SKETCHBOOK OF THE CIVIL WAR, Alexander Gardner. 100 photos taken on field during the Civil War. Famous shots of Manassas Harper's Ferry, Lincoln, Richmond, slave pens, etc. 244pp. 10⅝ x 8¼. 22731-6 Pa. $10.95

FIVE ACRES AND INDEPENDENCE, Maurice G. Kains. Great back-to-the-land classic explains basics of self-sufficient farming. The one book to get. 95 illustrations. 397pp. 5⅜ x 8½. 20974-1 Pa. $7.95

SONGS OF EASTERN BIRDS, Dr. Donald J. Borror. Songs and calls of 60 species most common to eastern U.S.: warblers, woodpeckers, flycatchers, thrushes, larks, many more in high-quality recording. Cassette and manual 99912-2 $9.95

A MODERN HERBAL, Margaret Grieve. Much the fullest, most exact, most useful compilation of herbal material. Gigantic alphabetical encyclopedia, from aconite to zedoary, gives botanical information, medical properties, folklore, economic uses, much else. Indispensable to serious reader. 161 illustrations. 888pp. 6½ x 9¼. 2-vol. set. (USO) Vol. I: 22798-7 Pa. $9.95
Vol. II: 22799-5 Pa. $9.95

HIDDEN TREASURE MAZE BOOK, Dave Phillips. Solve 34 challenging mazes accompanied by heroic tales of adventure. Evil dragons, people-eating plants, blood-thirsty giants, many more dangerous adversaries lurk at every twist and turn. 34 mazes, stories, solutions. 48pp. 8¼ x 11. 24566-7 Pa. $2.95

LETTERS OF W. A. MOZART, Wolfgang A. Mozart. Remarkable letters show bawdy wit, humor, imagination, musical insights, contemporary musical world; includes some letters from Leopold Mozart. 276pp. 5⅜ x 8½. 22859-2 Pa. $7.95

BASIC PRINCIPLES OF CLASSICAL BALLET, Agrippina Vaganova. Great Russian theoretician, teacher explains methods for teaching classical ballet. 118 illustrations. 175pp. 5⅜ x 8½. 22036-2 Pa. $5.95

THE JUMPING FROG, Mark Twain. Revenge edition. The original story of The Celebrated Jumping Frog of Calaveras County, a hapless French translation, and Twain's hilarious "retranslation" from the French. 12 illustrations. 66pp. 5⅜ x 8½. 22686-7 Pa. $3.95

BEST REMEMBERED POEMS, Martin Gardner (ed.). The 126 poems in this superb collection of 19th- and 20th-century British and American verse range from Shelley's "To a Skylark" to the impassioned "Renascence" of Edna St. Vincent Millay and to Edward Lear's whimsical "The Owl and the Pussycat." 224pp. 5⅜ x 8½. 27165-X Pa. $5.95

COMPLETE SONNETS, William Shakespeare. Over 150 exquisite poems deal with love, friendship, the tyranny of time, beauty's evanescence, death and other themes in language of remarkable power, precision and beauty. Glossary of archaic terms. 80pp. 5³⁄₁₆ x 8¼. 26686-9 Pa. $1.00

BODIES IN A BOOKSHOP, R. T. Campbell. Challenging mystery of blackmail and murder with ingenious plot and superbly drawn characters. In the best tradition of British suspense fiction. 192pp. 5⅜ x 8½. 24720-1 Pa. $6.95

CATALOG OF DOVER BOOKS

THE WIT AND HUMOR OF OSCAR WILDE, Alvin Redman (ed.). More than 1,000 ripostes, paradoxes, wisecracks: Work is the curse of the drinking classes; I can resist everything except temptation; etc. 258pp. 5⅜ x 8½. 20602-5 Pa. $6.95

SHAKESPEARE LEXICON AND QUOTATION DICTIONARY, Alexander Schmidt. Full definitions, locations, shades of meaning in every word in plays and poems. More than 50,000 exact quotations. 1,485pp. 6½ x 9¼. 2-vol. set.
Vol. 1: 22726-X Pa. $17.95
Vol. 2: 22727-8 Pa. $17.95

SELECTED POEMS, Emily Dickinson. Over 100 best-known, best-loved poems by one of America's foremost poets, reprinted from authoritative early editions. No comparable edition at this price. Index of first lines. 64pp. 5³⁄₁₆ x 8¼.
26466-1 Pa. $1.00

THE INSIDIOUS DR. FU-MANCHU, Sax Rohmer. The first of the popular mystery series introduces a pair of English detectives to their archnemesis, the diabolical Dr. Fu-Manchu. Flavorful atmosphere, fast-paced action, and colorful characters enliven this classic of the genre. 208pp. 5³⁄₁₆ x 8¼. 29898-1 Pa. $2.00

THE MALLEUS MALEFICARUM OF KRAMER AND SPRENGER, translated by Montague Summers. Full text of most important witchhunter's "bible," used by both Catholics and Protestants. 278pp. 6⅝ x 10. 22802-9 Pa. $12.95

SPANISH STORIES/CUENTOS ESPAÑOLES: A Dual-Language Book, Angel Flores (ed.). Unique format offers 13 great stories in Spanish by Cervantes, Borges, others. Faithful English translations on facing pages. 352pp. 5⅜ x 8½.
25399-6 Pa. $8.95

GARDEN CITY, LONG ISLAND, IN EARLY PHOTOGRAPHS, 1869–1919, Mildred H. Smith. Handsome treasury of 118 vintage pictures, accompanied by carefully researched captions, document the Garden City Hotel fire (1899), the Vanderbilt Cup Race (1908), the first airmail flight departing from the Nassau Boulevard Aerodrome (1911), and much more. 96pp. 8⅞ x 11¾. 40669-5 Pa. $12.95

OLD QUEENS, N.Y., IN EARLY PHOTOGRAPHS, Vincent F. Seyfried and William Asadorian. Over 160 rare photographs of Maspeth, Jamaica, Jackson Heights, and other areas. Vintage views of DeWitt Clinton mansion, 1939 World's Fair and more. Captions. 192pp. 8⅞ x 11. 26358-4 Pa. $12.95

CAPTURED BY THE INDIANS: 15 Firsthand Accounts, 1750-1870, Frederick Drimmer. Astounding true historical accounts of grisly torture, bloody conflicts, relentless pursuits, miraculous escapes and more, by people who lived to tell the tale. 384pp. 5⅜ x 8½. 24901-8 Pa. $8.95

THE WORLD'S GREAT SPEECHES (Fourth Enlarged Edition), Lewis Copeland, Lawrence W. Lamm, and Stephen J. McKenna. Nearly 300 speeches provide public speakers with a wealth of updated quotes and inspiration—from Pericles' funeral oration and William Jennings Bryan's "Cross of Gold Speech" to Malcolm X's powerful words on the Black Revolution and Earl of Spenser's tribute to his sister, Diana, Princess of Wales. 944pp. 5⅜ x 8⅜. 40903-1 Pa. $15.95

THE BOOK OF THE SWORD, Sir Richard F. Burton. Great Victorian scholar/adventurer's eloquent, erudite history of the "queen of weapons"—from prehistory to early Roman Empire. Evolution and development of early swords, variations (sabre, broadsword, cutlass, scimitar, etc.), much more. 336pp. 6⅛ x 9¼.
25434-8 Pa. $9.95

AUTOBIOGRAPHY: The Story of My Experiments with Truth, Mohandas K. Gandhi. Boyhood, legal studies, purification, the growth of the Satyagraha (nonviolent protest) movement. Critical, inspiring work of the man responsible for the freedom of India. 480pp. 5⅜ x 8½. (USO)   24593-4 Pa. $8.95

CELTIC MYTHS AND LEGENDS, T. W. Rolleston. Masterful retelling of Irish and Welsh stories and tales. Cuchulain, King Arthur, Deirdre, the Grail, many more. First paperback edition. 58 full-page illustrations. 512pp. 5⅜ x 8½.   26507-2 Pa. $9.95

THE PRINCIPLES OF PSYCHOLOGY, William James. Famous long course complete, unabridged. Stream of thought, time perception, memory, experimental methods; great work decades ahead of its time. 94 figures. 1,391pp. 5⅜ x 8½. 2-vol. set.
Vol. I: 20381-6 Pa. $13.95
Vol. II: 20382-4 Pa. $14.95

THE WORLD AS WILL AND REPRESENTATION, Arthur Schopenhauer. Definitive English translation of Schopenhauer's life work, correcting more than 1,000 errors, omissions in earlier translations. Translated by E. F. J. Payne. Total of 1,269pp. 5⅜ x 8½. 2-vol. set.   Vol. 1: 21761-2 Pa. $12.95
Vol. 2: 21762-0 Pa. $12.95

MAGIC AND MYSTERY IN TIBET, Madame Alexandra David-Neel. Experiences among lamas, magicians, sages, sorcerers, Bonpa wizards. A true psychic discovery. 32 illustrations. 321pp. 5⅜ x 8½. (USO)   22682-4 Pa. $9.95

THE EGYPTIAN BOOK OF THE DEAD, E. A. Wallis Budge. Complete reproduction of Ani's papyrus, finest ever found. Full hieroglyphic text, interlinear transliteration, word-for-word translation, smooth translation. 533pp. 6½ x 9¼.
21866-X Pa. $11.95

MATHEMATICS FOR THE NONMATHEMATICIAN, Morris Kline. Detailed, college-level treatment of mathematics in cultural and historical context, with numerous exercises. Recommended Reading Lists. Tables. Numerous figures. 641pp. 5⅜ x 8½.
24823-2 Pa. $11.95

PROBABILISTIC METHODS IN THE THEORY OF STRUCTURES, Isaac Elishakoff. Well-written introduction covers the elements of the theory of probability from two or more random variables, the reliability of such multivariable structures, the theory of random function, Monte Carlo methods of treating problems incapable of exact solution, and more. Examples. 502pp. 5³⁄₈ x 8¹⁄₂.   40691-1 Pa. $16.95

THE RIME OF THE ANCIENT MARINER, Gustave Doré, S. T. Coleridge. Doré's finest work; 34 plates capture moods, subtleties of poem. Flawless full-size reproductions printed on facing pages with authoritative text of poem. "Beautiful. Simply beautiful."–*Publisher's Weekly.* 77pp. 9¼ x 12.   22305-1 Pa. $7.95

NORTH AMERICAN INDIAN DESIGNS FOR ARTISTS AND CRAFTSPEOPLE, Eva Wilson. Over 360 authentic copyright-free designs adapted from Navajo blankets, Hopi pottery, Sioux buffalo hides, more. Geometrics, symbolic figures, plant and animal motifs, etc. 128pp. 8⅜ x 11. (EUK)   25341-4 Pa. $8.95

SCULPTURE: Principles and Practice, Louis Slobodkin. Step-by-step approach to clay, plaster, metals, stone; classical and modern. 253 drawings, photos. 255pp. 8⅛ x 11.
22960-2 Pa. $11.95

THE INFLUENCE OF SEA POWER UPON HISTORY, 1660–1783, A. T. Mahan. Influential classic of naval history and tactics still used as text in war colleges. First paperback edition. 4 maps. 24 battle plans. 640pp. 5⅜ x 8½.   25509-3 Pa. $14.95

THE STORY OF THE TITANIC AS TOLD BY ITS SURVIVORS, Jack Winocour (ed.). What it was really like. Panic, despair, shocking inefficiency, and a little heroism. More thrilling than any fictional account. 26 illustrations. 320pp. 5⅜ x 8½.
20610-6 Pa. $8.95

FAIRY AND FOLK TALES OF THE IRISH PEASANTRY, William Butler Yeats (ed.). Treasury of 64 tales from the twilight world of Celtic myth and legend: "The Soul Cages," "The Kildare Pooka," "King O'Toole and his Goose," many more. Introduction and Notes by W. B. Yeats. 352pp. 5⅜ x 8½.   26941-8 Pa. $8.95

BUDDHIST MAHAYANA TEXTS, E. B. Cowell and Others (eds.). Superb, accurate translations of basic documents in Mahayana Buddhism, highly important in history of religions. The Buddha-karita of Asvaghosha, Larger Sukhavativyuha, more. 448pp. 5⅜ x 8½.   25552-2 Pa. $12.95

ONE TWO THREE . . . INFINITY: Facts and Speculations of Science, George Gamow. Great physicist's fascinating, readable overview of contemporary science: number theory, relativity, fourth dimension, entropy, genes, atomic structure, much more. 128 illustrations. Index. 352pp. 5⅜ x 8½.   25664-2 Pa. $8.95

EXPERIMENTATION AND MEASUREMENT, W. J. Youden. Introductory manual explains laws of measurement in simple terms and offers tips for achieving accuracy and minimizing errors. Mathematics of measurement, use of instruments, experimenting with machines. 1994 edition. Foreword. Preface. Introduction. Epilogue. Selected Readings. Glossary. Index. Tables and figures. 128pp. $5^3/_8$ x $8^1/_2$.
40451-X Pa. $6.95

DALÍ ON MODERN ART: The Cuckolds of Antiquated Modern Art, Salvador Dalí. Influential painter skewers modern art and its practitioners. Outrageous evaluations of Picasso, Cézanne, Turner, more. 15 renderings of paintings discussed. 44 calligraphic decorations by Dalí. 96pp. 5⅜ x 8½. (USO)   29220-7 Pa. $5.95

ANTIQUE PLAYING CARDS: A Pictorial History, Henry René D'Allemagne. Over 900 elaborate, decorative images from rare playing cards (14th–20th centuries): Bacchus, death, dancing dogs, hunting scenes, royal coats of arms, players cheating, much more. 96pp. 9¼ x 12¼.   29265-7 Pa. $12.95

MAKING FURNITURE MASTERPIECES: 30 Projects with Measured Drawings, Franklin H. Gottshall. Step-by-step instructions, illustrations for constructing handsome, useful pieces, among them a Sheraton desk, Chippendale chair, Spanish desk, Queen Anne table and a William and Mary dressing mirror. 224pp. 8⅛ x 11¼.
29338-6 Pa. $13.95

THE FOSSIL BOOK: A Record of Prehistoric Life, Patricia V. Rich et al. Profusely illustrated definitive guide covers everything from single-celled organisms and dinosaurs to birds and mammals and the interplay between climate and man. Over 1,500 illustrations. 760pp. 7½ x 10⅛.   29371-8 Pa. $29.95